BRITISH BUSINESS
BUSINESS
AND
GHANAIAN
INDEPENDENCE

by

JOSEPHINE F. MILBURN

Published for the University of Rhode Island by
THE UNIVERSITY PRESS OF NEW ENGLAND
Hanover, New Hampshire, 1977

The University Press of New England

Brandeis University
Clark University
Dartmouth College
University of New Hampshire
University of Rhode Island
University of Vermont

BRITISH BUSINESS AND
GHANAIAN INDEPENDENCE

CONTENTS

TABLES

PREFACE

In the Gold Coast a period of dynamic development gained momentum in the late 1930's and led ultimately, in 1957, to independence. During this time various British businesses were actively engaged in trading and in cocoa marketing. It is natural to ask if British business played a significant role in the economic and political developments of the period. The focus of the present volume is on this question, and on an equally significant question, namely, the role of British business in decisions of the Colonial Office.

In this connection the study includes an analysis of the relations between British business operating in the Gold Coast and the Colonial Office in London, an evaluation of the business role in the development of this new country, and descriptions of the reception of business in the Gold Coast by African leaders, government officials, and Colonial officials. There follows an assessment of various characterizations of British business in West African development. In the main these evaluations are based upon materials made available by officials from the British businesses, the former colonial service, and the Ghanaian government.

The present study afforded the author a unique opportunity to combine concerns with British interest in politics with those of African Commonwealth affairs. The investigations arose mainly from efforts to understand the involvement of business in governmental administration—an area yet to receive detailed scrutiny in Britain. Among material already available on this topic is a discussion of the relation of business to government in Britain in J. P. D. Stewart's volume on British pressure groups.[1] Before Stewart's work, publications on British interests were concerned particularly with labor, the unions, and the political process. More recently, interest studies have continued with examination of such groups as teachers, veterans, and various federations.[2] Considerable work remains to be done on the involvement of interests in the British political process and especially in the administrative process. A major difficulty with such investigations is the thirty years' restriction on use of governmental records in Britain. For studies of administrative processes after the middle 1940's the researcher must therefore rely heavily on group records, interviews, and such public documents as white papers and Commission reports.

Within the Commonwealth African countries, Ghana was chosen for the central focus of this investigation primarily for two reasons:

Preface

(1) The Gold Coast was the first black African state to achieve independence after the Second World War, and compared to many other African states, its transition seems relatively smooth; therefore it seemed likely that records concerning the drive toward independence would have been preserved by both business and governmental bodies; (2) During the last twenty years before independence, there were a number of governmental commissions which had brought into public view information that could be used to analyze the relations between business and the Colonial Office.

Major sources for these analyses include public documents and newspapers; the records of the British firms, particularly the United Africa Company (UAC), Cadbury and Sons (Cadburys), and John Holt, Liverpool (Holts),[3] reports of these firms to the Colonial Office and the Gold Coast Administration; and interviews in England and Ghana with former colonial officials, Ghanaians involved in these affairs, and business personnel. A large portion of the business records and testimonies to governmental commissions were first made available for this study.

A number of commissions, appointed by the British government, dealt with affairs of concern to British business before 1957. These included the Commissions of Enquiry on the Marketing of West African Cocoa (*Report*, Cmd. 5845, 1938) and into Disturbances in the Gold Coast in 1948 (*Report*, Colonial No. 231). The Colonial Office also issued white papers on the future of marketing boards in 1944 and 1946 (Cmds. 6554 and 6950). After the Second World War the Gold Coast government appointed a number of committees and commissions of enquiry on such problem areas as wartime controls, africanisation of the civil service, development programs, mining concessions, and banking problems. The records of the firms' presentations to these commissions and committees vary in completeness. They were made available either from the firms' archives or from the personal collections of the firms' personnel who handled the testimonies.

Without the assistance of numerous people in Great Britain, Ghana, and the United States over the past ten years, this study would not have been possible. I owe a debt of gratitude to all who helped. Many are mentioned in the text among the approximately two hundred people who shared with me their knowledge about these events. In addition to those associated with business, the Colonial Office, and government during the period of investigation, I should like to thank various university people in Oxford, London, Cambridge, and Ghana for insights about these developments. Particular thanks go to Professor Max Beloff, who was my adviser while at Oxford; Thomas Hodgkin, who gave advice about various aspects of the work in Ghana; Professor Kenneth Robinson, who encouraged me to analyze business and Colonial Office relations from 1938; Professor C. H. Wilson, who discussed at length aspects of the United Africa Company activities; Professor Dennis Austin, who has given advice throughout the study; the librarians at Rhodes House and at the Colonial Records Project in Oxford; the Archivist at the Government Archives in Accra; former colonial officers now in England, Ghana, and New Zealand; and the librarians at the University libraries in London, Oxford, Legon, Kumasi, Greater Boston, Kingston (Rhode Island), and Providence. All remain in my memory because of their genuine interest and desire to assist. Reviewing and editorial assistance from the publisher, from Naomi F. Zucker of Kingston, Rhode Island, from Richard Hill and William Mazika of the University of Rhode Island, and from Anani Dzidzienyo of Brown University contributed immensely to the preparation of the volume, for which I also record my sincere thanks.

The research for the study was made possible by grants from the National Science Foundation for work during a year in England (1965–66), from the American Philosophical Society for work in England and in Ghana in 1966, and from the Simmons College Research Fund for work during the summers of 1967 and 1968.

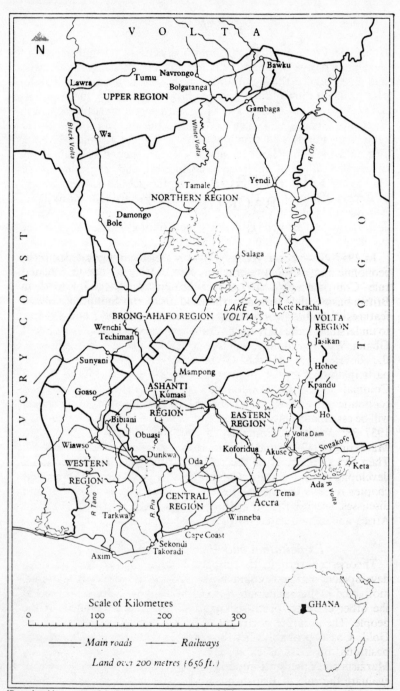

V O L T A

N

Lawra
Tumu
Navrongo
Bawku
Bolgatanga
UPPER REGION
Gambaga

Black Volta
Wa
White Volta
R Oti

Tamale
Yendi
NORTHERN REGION

Damongo
Bole

Salaga

LAKE
VOLTA
Kete Krachi
VOLTA
REGION

BRONG-AHAFO REGION
Wenchi
Techiman
Jasikan

Sunyani
Hohoe
Kpandu

Goaso
Mampong
ASHANTI
Kumasi
REGION
EASTERN
REGION
Ho

Bibiani
Obuasi
Volta Dam

Wiawso
Dunkwa
Koforidua
Akuse
Sogakofe

Oda
Keta

WESTERN
REGION
R Tano
R Pra
CENTRAL
REGIÓN
Ada
R Volta

Tarkwa
Tema

Winneba
Accra

Cape Coast
Sekondi
Takoradi

Axim

I V O R Y   C O A S T

T O G O

Scale of Kilometres

0   100   200   300

⎯⎯⎯ *Main roads*   ⎯+⎯ *Railways*

Land over 200 metres (656 ft.)

GHANA

GHANA

1

THE APPROACH AND THE BACKGROUND

In 1957 Ghana emerged as a nation seeking independence from economic and political restrictions fostered during British colonial rule. Contributing to the market and economic conditions were British businesses involved in trade and cocoa marketing. Two major features of the business role will be critically analyzed as we attempt to understand more fully the political and economic developments of Ghana. We will examine, first, the specific role of British business in the development of the Ghanaian market, and second, the participation of British business in certain decisions of the British Colonial Office in London affecting Ghanaian political and economic moves toward nationhood. The approach to each aspect will be essentially chronological. Emphasis is on the Cocoa Hold-Up 1937–38; Wartime Controls of 1939–45; Prices, Supply, and Marketing, 1947–48; and Africanisation and Development, 1948–57. Then follow analyses of the role of British business in economic development and certain Colonial Office decisions. The present chapter reviews theories about business in developing nations and discusses, specific British businesses associated with trade in West Africa and some related historic trends.

Exploitation and Humanitarian Aspects

Theories concerning the impact of business on West African development variously characterize business as, at the one extreme, motivated by humanitarian concerns in economic decisions, and at the other extreme, profit-seeking capitalists and exploiters of the people. The accurate portrayal of British business activities on the Gold Coast probably lies somewhere between these extreme positions. Business as exploitation was advanced particularly by Marxists and other anti-imperialists. One aim of this study is to re-evaluate the role of British business in West Africa, placing these generally popular views about business in perspective on the basis of the evidence at hand.

1

It is fairly clear that from 1937 to 1957, British firms were active in economic development of the Gold Coast. The extent of their activities varied from firm to firm: some firms participated only in trade and the setting of trade policy, others lent assistance to educational and social development and participated in the formulation of government policies. But several questions remain to be answered: to what extent did the firms take action and make changes through their own initiative, and to what extent through government suggestion and instigation? Were their investments in trade, commerce, and industry of considerable aid to economic activities? Did they accelerate the move toward political independence?

Definitions of "capitalism"; "exploitation", and "innovation" as used herein may be useful. "Capitalism" is used in a very general and popular sense to refer to a system in which enterprises are concerned mainly with obtaining profits from their operations; it is not used in the restricted sense of Adam Smith, and it will include businesses tending toward monopolistic forms and those controlled by governmental measures. "Exploitation" is used to refer to a system in which business firms remove all or almost all profits from the country in which they have invested, benefiting the country little, if at all. "Innovation" will refer to a system in which business firms, along with maintaining their economic enterprises, initiate economic and sometime social change in the country of investment, thus bringing economic and/or social benefits to the internal society.

The spectrum of views about British business in the Gold Coast includes that of the conspiratorial nature of business. Such views were frequently voiced in missionary writings and in critiques on the colonial and imperial systems. Lenin described the last stage of capitalism as imperialism, which to him was "finance capitalism" in which finance for development was exported to new areas. According to Hobson, imperialism involving investments in foreign land results in expenditures of public money on ships, guns, and the military, and thus leads to profits of war.[1]

Nkrumah, in his book on neocolonialism published just before the 1966 coup in Ghana, describes as "imperialist finance" the activities of various concerns, such as the United Africa Company (UAC) and Consolidated African Selection Trust (CAST). "Incredibly", he asserts, "the list [in a recent survey] leaves out two of the world's greatest combines, those states within a state—Unilever and Imperial Chemical Industries (I.C.I.) whose operations are based heavily in their overseas exploitations. The United Africa Company leads for Unilever in Africa; about a third of I.C.I. and its subsidiaries operate overseas".[2] Fitch and Oppenheimer further examined, in 1966, neocolonial developments.

Green and Seidman describe the UAC in Africa as a company

"that ships the bulk of its products in raw form to be processed in Britain and Europe where it has put over 50% of its investment in processing plants". Of the new Unilever efforts to enter more into the production of consumer goods, they say that these ventures are not designed primarily to build basic industry or to free Africa . . . but rather "to employ low cost African labour to process some raw materials or to assemble and package semi-finished materials, much of them imported, for sale in the largest African markets". Yet "UAC is an exception" to most foreign firms, as "most will not invest outside their 'own' fields".[3]

Some variations on the conspiratorial view appear to present business in a less objectionable role. Quaison–Sackey explained recently that European traders and missionaries had been in the Gold Coast before colonialism began. In this connection he pointed out that European education was introduced through these groups and that colonialism was thus not necessary to bring intercourse between the European and the Ghanaian.[4] Godfrey Lardner of the United Nations Economic Commission for Africa, research and planning division, and Kafo Apeadu of the Regional Economic Co-operation Divisions of the same Commission, discussed development during the sixties and seventies. Mr. Lardner stated:

Much of the industry in African countries is simply an extension of some advanced country's domestic economy. But even where industry has grown, there has been a slowing down because of the concentration on import-substitution affecting a miscellany of products. Industry must have an organic, related structure, so import-substitution of nonrelated products has soon run out of steam.

Mr. Apeadu then points out what was done and what needs to be done to develop the countries further. He emphasizes regional development as the only course for further economic development in the seventies.[5]

Other views of the motives of business were offered throughout the course of West African development by the British Colonial administration. At times divergent views of business were expressed by the Colonial Office in London and the Coast administration. These are discussed in later chapters.

The Business Concerns

In this study of British business interests in West Africa, concentration is upon the interrelations between the Colonial Office and three British firms: United Africa Company, Cadbury Brothers Limited, and John Holt and Company (Liverpool). The study does not pursue in detail the activities of various federations of British businesses, mainly because the British federations were little concerned with West African affairs. UAC, Cadburys, and Holts were chosen for their prominence in West African trade for a considerable portion of the period from 1900, because of the diversity of their activities on the Coast, and because of their involvement in the cocoa crisis of 1937–38. Although the three firms enjoyed a common concern with buying cocoa for the world market, each represented a different type of operation: UAC was the largest supplier of merchandise on the Coast in the thirties and forties, and in later years it started new economic enterprises, such as an export operation in timber and breweries for local consumption; Holts, with somewhat similar interests but smaller investments in Ghana, acted as a supplier of various types of goods and services; and Cadburys has continued primarily as a chocolate manufacturer, with its main plants in England.

UAC in the 1930's was one of the largest merchandise firms on the Gold Coast and before Ghanaian independence had one of the most extensive business operations. It was formed in 1929 from the merger of the Niger Company and the African and Eastern Trade Corporation. In 1931 the company acquired Unilever's West African holdings, and by 1938 had assimilated six commercial and industrial enterprises. At that time UAC reported a capital of £11,000,000 in ordinary shares. Lever Brothers held 80 percent and the African and Eastern Trade Corporation held 20 percent of these shares. During the 1936–37 season, UAC purchased from 8 to 10 thousand tons of cocoa in the Gold Coast.[6] After the Second World War UAC continued with active trading on the Coast, and until today it has maintained investments through redeployment of its operations to adjust to the changes in the Ghanaian economy.

The merchandise firm of Holts was organized in the 1860's but it did not enter the Gold Coast cocoa trade until 1935.[7] This trade constituted only a small part of the company's operations. When Holts first came to the Gold Coast, it intended to buy cocoa for cash only. To establish trade, however, permission was given to "cut into [their] buying and establishment charges, so that in reality [they] were paying more than the ruling market price. This practice did not allow the organisation to buy, however, but in fact only to exist in the buying system because of the previous practice to retain brokers".[8] As a newcomer in the thirties, Holts was particularly affected by market conditions and not long after the movement for independence began to limit its activities on the Coast. Today its main Ghanaian involvement is in the area of motors and motor services.

Cadburys, a British cocoa manufacturing firm, was involved in coastal trade as early as 1908 because of its need for raw cocoa. In 1918 merger arrangements were started with J. S. Fry and Sons, and from 1930 to 1936 the firm bought cocoa for other firms, such as Rowntree. During the 1930's Cadburys worked for improvements in the cultivation and preparation of cocoa, frequently meeting with officials of the Colonial Office and the local administration. These interests have continued until the present.[9]

Some attention is also given to two mining concerns: Ashanti Goldfields, noted for its personal and long-standing contracts with British colonial officials and later with officials in the Gold Coast and Ghanaian governments, and the Consolidated African Selection Trust, which in 1931 took over the African Selection Trust operations in the Gold Coast for which concessions had been granted in the twenties. The customary land tenure arrangements differed from one district to another, and these conditioned the kind of European holdings possible on the Coast. Mining rights were usually arranged on a lease basis with chiefs, and European settlers were not encouraged, since the European concept of ownership differed from normal practices on the Coast.[10] In 1938 there were three diamond companies in the Birim district, including CAST and the Holland Syndicate.[11] By 1950, diamond production in some years was exceeding one million carats.

The banks, though important, are given only brief attention because of their lack of involvement with the main commissions under scrutiny and because of the difficulty in finding sources related to their governmental contracts.

Only a few British business federations have played a part in the development of the Gold Coast economy.[12] Those with some involvement were the Joint West Africa Committee, the Association of Cocoa Manufacturers, and the Association of West African Merchants, business organizations operating in West Africa at various times before and during the period of concern in this volume.

The Joint West Africa Committee, first formed in 1902 and reconstituted in 1956 as the West Africa Committee, was a loose confederation of the West African Sections of the London, Liverpool and Manchester Chambers of Commerce.[13] Throughout its history the Committee not only sent communications to the Colonial Office in London, but also arranged meetings with appropriate Colonial officials whenever it was thought necessary.[14]

The Association of West African Merchants (AWAM)[15] became, through governmental prescription during the Second World War, important in the determination of prices and quotas for trading goods on the Coast and in London. It was the focus of considerable criticism and hostility in the late forties as the culprit in forcing high prices, affected trade on the Coast and governmental policy.

Some Historical Trends

Dramatic transitions are still in progress in West Africa, including those associated with the movement from rural to urban living. All facets of life continue to be affected.[16] Here we shall concentrate on politcical and economic events prior to 1938.

The first Englishman to reach the Gold Coast, according to reports, was a trader who arrived in 1555.[17] Some hundred years later, British trading companies, involved until 1807 in the slave trade, began to go to Cape Coast. The first significant one in the trade was in 1660, the Company of Royal Adventurers, and this was replaced successively in 1672 by the Royal African Company and in 1750 by the African Company of Merchants. In 1821 the Committee of London Merchants took over trade on the Gold Coast. The administration of George MacLean, also president of the local Merchants Council from 1830 to 1844, brought to the Coast, according to some histories, efficient administration and some peace and prosperity.[18]

In 1874 the British government assumed control over coastal affairs. The primary goal of the government at that time appeared to be to protect the territory during the scramble for Africa, which most frequently meant protecting the trading firms when the companies so requested. The Government also maintained contact with various African groups, including the Ashanti of the middle Kumasi area, and the Ga, Akan, and Ewes of the Eastern Province; and among other activities it struggled to settle problems of land ownership. When in 1873 the British Government took over Elmina and other Dutch forts, the Ashanti objected, and the British soon sent troops to Kumasi. Open hostilities came to a halt with the Treaty of Fomena. In 1895 the Government sent an expedition to Kumasi to establish a protectorate. Even though the Ashanti during the following year submitted, their Asantehene (Paramount Chief) was deported.[19] Prempeh I was held for a time at Elmina before being sent to the Seychelles Islands.

In 1901 the Colonial Office took over the territories now making up Ghana. District Commissioners were appointed in the Ashanti Division and in the Northern Territories. The Western and Eastern Provinces were created later, in 1927, from the Ashanti Division, but Ashanti members were not brought into the Legislative Council until 1946. Some Africans had served since 1920 on the reconstituted Legislative Council, but until the 1930's there was little concern about self-government except in the Coastal cities, probably because the Colonial Office in the hinterland of the Gold Coast continued to use African rulers to administer directives.

The first governor to demonstrate active concern about the education of the African and his participation in government was Sir Gordon Guggisberg (1919–27). Guggisberg's plan for education included the establishment of Achimota College in 1925. There were missionary schools on the secondary level before but no government financed secondary schools. He also initiated a constitution that provided for fourteen unofficial members of the Legislative Council—nine African and Five Europeans. Three Africans were elected in the towns, while six were paramount chiefs elected by the provincial councils of the three provinces (also provided for in the constitution).

During World War Two and again just after the war, Sir Alan Burns, Governor from 1941 to 1946, reactivated the recommendations of Guggisberg for further Africanisation of the government. He urged that more Africans be brought into the administration of the Colony, and initiated a new constitution, adopted in 1946, which provided for increased African representation in the Legislative Council. Provision was made for the election of eighteen members and for the appointment of six members including representatives of Chambers of Commerce and Mines. There were also six ex-officio members and a President appointed by the Governor.[20] An African majority on the Assembly was thus provided through the elected members.

Sir Alan Burns, in each message to the Legislative Council, expressed concern for the economic and social need of the people. Notably, in his February 23 speech on the 1943–44 budget, he enumerated educational, medical, and economic problems and suggested solutions. Although he did not directly consult the British firms on these issues, he did consider their suggestions when they were made.[21]

Following World War Two and with the return of servicemen, the problems of unemployment and a scarcity of goods provoked general discontent, which led to demonstrations in several Gold Coast cities. After Gerald Creasy took office as the new Governor, in January 1948, ex-servicemen requested permission to march in Accra on February 28 and to present a petition to the Governor at Christianborg Castle (Government House). Permission to march to the Governor's Castle was refused. When the police delineated the march route away from the Castle there was resistance. The police sergeant in charge fired on the marchers after they departed from the route and refused to return. Some bullets hit marchers. (Sergeant Ajetey's death occurred where the arch known as Independence Monument is located.) Riots resulted, which led to wider unrest and looting in the business areas of Accra, and later to disturbances in other towns.[22] A Commission of Enquiry (known as the Watson Commission) was dispatched from London to examine the causes of the disturbances and to suggest measures to alleviate the problems. A major recommendation of the Watson Commission was that measures be taken to increase self-government in the Gold Coast. As a result, a constitutional commission was appointed, with an African as chairman. This was the first governmental commission to be chaired by a Gold Coaster. He was Henley Coussey, a judge of the High Court. The Commission reported in 1949 and a new constitution came into effect in 1950. The Convention People's Party members had boycotted the Coussey Commission and had refused to give testimony. Dr. Nkrumah returned from London in January 1948 to become general secretary of the United Gold Coast Convention (which was dissolved after the 1951 elections). In June 1949 Nkrumah formed the main nationalist party—the CPP. Despite the Convention People's Party's view of the commission as "bogus and fraudulent". It was under this constitution that Nkrumah became Leader of Government Business in 1951 and Prime Minister in 1952.

Self-government was now established on the Coast in an essentially parliamentary system, with provisions for a government to be formed from the majority party in the legislature. The Legislative Assembly was composed of 84 members, 75 of whom were elected (an increase of 57 over the previous 18). This parliament existed primarily to advise the Governor through the Prime Minister. A Cabinet of 11 was to be responsible to the Assembly and the Governor. By 1950 the administration had increased the number of African civil servants, yet not sufficiently to avert another study of Africanisation in the Civil Service. (Earlier studies had been made by Governor Gordon Guggisberg in the twenties and Governor Alan Burns in the forties.) The Commission issued its report in 1951.

Trends toward urbanization on the Coast had been evident since the turn of the century. An increase from 20,000 to 600,000 people from 1901 to 1966 illustrates the rise in population in Accra. Migration was one major source of the increase.[23] Naturally the burgeoning city population brought needs for housing, education, and health services. During the nineteenth century most European-type educational and welfare provisions had come from missionary efforts. Moving into the twentieth century, the colonial government began to place more emphasis on educational needs and health concerns, although there was insufficient activity to keep ahead of the problems. Up to 1939 little effort had gone into sanitation and housing in urban areas despite the increased migration to cities. The Gold Coast budget for education increased from £54,442 in 1919 to £270,000 in 1938. In real terms, taking account of inflation, this would be equivalent in British funds to almost a 50 percent increase. Achimota College, the first governmentally financed school, started in 1925, was opened for secondary school training by 1931. Medical care by 1939 included 38 African hospitals and some mission hospitals,[24] and additional provisions for education and health were made in the forties and fifties. Facilities continued to improve through the sixties, yet with continued migration to the cities the provisions for social services were still insufficient.[25]

The major sources of revenue for programs in the Gold Coast were export taxes on minerals and cocoa. In addition, the British government began to support projects in the colonies through special funds, including the Colonial Development Funds first authorized in the 1920's. The Colonial Office, authorized by Parliament in 1939, increased the funds from £5 million for the first ten years (1925–35) to £5 million per year.[26] The Gold Coast received some financial assistance in the 1930's, mainly to meet rising budgets in education and health, but it received little direct support from these funds in later years.[27]

Industrialization within the Gold Coast occurred mainly after the Second World War, first in the Volta River project, planning for which begun in 1942, and after 1957, through efforts of Nkrumah's government. Before the war, major developments included the construction of limited tonnage railroads and, in the twenties, the Takoradi harbour. Mining as early as 1897 was mainly under the control of British corporations.[28]

Commercial activities, which had begun in the nineteenth century, had grown considerably by the 1930's, mainly because of cocoa's development as a cash crop. Small-scale marketing activities have consistently been the concern of the African, but large-scale commercial activities were carried out largely by foreign merchandise companies. The United Africa Company and John Holt and Company (since 1938) have been among the largest British concerns buying cocoa and supplying goods in bulk to Ghana. With the advent in 1947 of a marketing board for cocoa, these concerns became agents for the government, transporting cocoa and selling it on the foreign market, while they continued to supply goods to the domestic market.

From 1947 the firms operated in the field until 1961 only if they were appointed as local buying agents. Cocoa was the property of the Board as soon as it was purchased, and the Board handled its sale overseas through the governmentally established Cocoa Marketing Company. Finally, as the Marketing Board and later the Cocoa Purchasing Company increased their power to buy and sell cocoa, the firms actively encouraged other activities that would be useful in the Ghanaian economy. Thus Holts began to supply the motor and machinery market, while UAC diversified its resources. The long-term investors found it easier to reinvest in activities on the Coast, while new investors found more difficulty in establishing long-term investments.

Agricultural produce, and particularly cocoa, occupied the attention of various Gold Coast and Ghanaian governments. Despite efforts to introduce some variety into the agricultural scene, cocoa has maintained its pre-eminence throughout the century. Its importance is apparent when compared with the export of kola nuts, coffee, palmed copra, shea nuts, bananas, and rubber for 1938, 1955, and 1960.[29] Today exports of minerals, especially gold and diamonds, and timber come next in the list of important products from Ghana.

Cocoa was first introduced into Ghana in 1857, reportedly by missionaries, but it was not until a Ghanaian goldsmith, Tetteh Kwashie, brought cocoa back from Fernando Po (Gulf of Guinea) in 1879 that cocoa began to be accepted as a crop.[29] Extraordinary changes in the export market from 1900 to 1936 resulted from the acceptance by the Gold Coast farmer of cocoa as a cash crop. Thus the annual tonnage over the period 1896 to 1900 was 329, while the annual average over the four-year period 1932 to 1936 was 256,033. The value of cocoa exports in 1906 was, according to J. D. Fage, £336,000, when for the first time cocoa brought in more than gold. In 1936 a record export of 311,151 tons, worth £7,660,000, made up 63 percent of the Gold Coast exports and supplied 43 percent of the world's supply. By 1938 the annual cocoa export was 263,000 tons, with a value of £4,541,000. Cocoa exports began to fall off after 1939 because of the effects of swollen shoot and the difficulties of the war period, but they increased again in 1955, when exports were 283,000 tons, and by 1960 they exceeded 400,000 tons. In 1965 crop purchases were 484,000 tons [30]

The 1965-66 season presented a major crisis for the Ghanaian economy. Cocoa prices had declined disastrously in 1964 and 1965, and some of the marketing Board's reserve funds, set aside in prosperous years from the farmers' earnings, had since 1961 been put into development funds. The Board was thus not prepared for a significant drop in world price. It was during this time that the February 1966 coup occurred. Again in 1970 the world price of cocoa declined, at a time when the recently elected constitutional government was introducing some developmental programs and economic controls unpopular with various sections of the society.

The role of British business and the Colonial Office in the affairs of the Gold Coast are, of course, most visible before the increased self-government provisions of the late forties. Our major investigations of these roles are therefore concerned largely with the period 1937–57, and consider the 1938 Cocoa Hold-Up, War-Time Controls, and, after the Second World War, Cocoa Marketing, the Disturbances, Africanisation, and Developmental activities.

2

THE 1938 COCOA CRISES

During the thirties, as noted, foreign-based business in the Gold Coast, according to general views on business, was thought to be engaged in exploitation for profits.[1] As early as 1930 foreign business was under scrutiny because of allegedly rigged prices.[2] Thus, when news of both a proposed arrangement between the firms buying cocoa and of the falling price of cocoa reached the farmers in 1937 at about the same time, they withheld cocoa from the market in the hope that prices would increase.

Kimble, an historian of the period, refers to patterns of exploitation when he describes trading in West Africa during the twenties and the Cocoa Hold-Up of 1930-31. In discussing the changes of price, however, he does not describe the firms as exploiters so much as scapegoats for the changes in world prices:

> It was not surprising that African primary producers, at the opposite economic pole, should come to distrust the operations of such large-scale expatriate enterprise. This was particularly true in the cocoa trade, where the known or suspected collusion between the merchants from time to time over buying prices brought upon them also the blame for world price movements which were beyond their control.[3]

A similar interpretation of the events seems applicable in 1937.

In descriptions of various produce crises in West Africa the Colonial Administrations have also received their share of criticism. In the first produce crisis of the nineteenth century, which resulted in an effective boycott of palm oil in 1858, the Colonial Administration was judged by Freda Wolfson to have lent positive support to the European merchants.[4] From descriptions of the 1938 crisis by W. K. Hancock and the 1938 Commission of Enquiry, she concludes that the Administration in contrast lent tacit support to the merchants through its passive attitude toward the crisis.[5]

Farmers, Brokers and Agents

Unlike the East African development of plantations for export crops, cocoa farming in British West Africa, including the Gold Coast, was left for the most part to the African farmer to develop.[6]

This was the case from the time cocoa was introduced. By the thirties the following practices had arisen: The crop was fermented and dried locally, and then sold to brokers. These brokers, who came to each farm to purchase the crop for the agents of British firms, were responsible ultimately for the price given to the farmer. The firms then transported the crop to the ports and thence to London, where it was sold at prices determined by the world market.[7]

In part this process involved the provision of advances from the firms to the brokers, and from the brokers to the farmers. These advances were acceptable to the farmers only as cash, and became a necessary part of the Coastal trade, since the farmers often needed funds to carry them before the cocoa harvest. The firms thus became responsible for sending, through British banks, large currency advances before the cocoa season began.[8]

The world market had two foci in 1937-38; New York and London. The New York market, because of its size, had a definite influence on the London market price. In this period most cocoa from West Africa was, however, sold on the London market. By 1930 contractual arrangements had developed for those dealing on each terminal market, and the futures market was certainly established in New York, as were private agreements about sales other than on the terminal markets in both centers. In London, Gill and Duffus has become the firm to which reference was made for prices of cocoa on the market and is still involved in the final transactions of selling cocoa on the London market to the manufactures.[9]

Colonial Policy during the 1930's

Decisions affecting the Gold Coast during the thirties were usually made by the Governor and his officials. District Commissioners also enjoyed considerable freedom in administering their respective areas. The lack of centralized control over policy interpretation and implementation was prevalent throughout the British Empire before the Second World War. A major reason included, of course, the great distances between London and the administrative centers and the length of time which long dispatches took to be delivered by ship. Cables were only used for brief communications during this period, but lengthy explanations of policy from London and replies from the Colonial administrations would usually travel by ship. Air mail was introduced between London and Accra in 1938, and only then did better communications between London and the Governor and between the Administration in Accra and the districts begin to develop. During most of the period covering the Cocoa Hold-Up, air mail was still not used, and communications were often sent by ship.

Even though details of policy directives tended to be slow in arriving, the Colonial Secretary would issue policy directives and explanations, as was the case relating to the firms' agreement on cocoa quotas in 1937. The Governor and his staff would then raise detailed objections to the implementation of these directives, as they did on the role of the Coastal Administration in explaining the firms' agreement. Much of this correspondence was by sea and the original directive from the Colonial Secretary was not implemented during the exchange of communications.[10]

This chapter reviews the relationships between British business and the Colonial Office in London, and between business and the Colonial Officials on the Coast. The proposed agreement on cocoa trade in 1937 will be the focus.

The Agreement

The price of Gold Coast cocoa reached a post-World War I high of £40 per ton during the 1936-37 season. Both the supply and price of cocoa had increased steadily after the 1930-31 hold-up, and in 1936 311,000 tons of cocoa valued at £7,760,000 were exported, yielding £363,000 in revenue derived from an export tax of £1 03s 04d per ton. During 1937, however, a depression on the world market, as evidenced by a drop of price, evoked concern among European buyers.[11]

Trade agreements of various types were not uncommon on the West Coast. Besides the palm oil attempt in 1858, later efforts to establish price agreements among the firms were made in 1916, 1921, and 1929. And cocoa, as already mentioned, was held up by the farmers in 1930-31.

Several British firms, including UAC, Holts, and Cadburys, were, in the spring and summer of 1937, exploring the possibilities of a marketing agreement to stabilize the price of cocoa.[12] Trade abuses—including misuse of large advances by the brokers who bought cocoa directly from the farmers to sell to the firms for overseas trading; irregularities in mortgages to the farmers and in providing securities for advances; the determination of the buying price on produce bought in advance of the season and without reference to world market price and other usual criteria; and faulty reporting on weights and on quality of the cocoa—all became more pronounced and required urgent attention.

UAC took the initiative in beginning discussions during the spring of 1937. Holts, also a buyer of cocoa and a seller of merchandise, entered the discussions because of its interest in arrangements for buying quotas among the firms. In the summer of 1937 Cadburys, a manufacturing firm buying cocoa, together with the other buyers (chiefly merchandise firms), also entered the discussions, because of their interest in controlling these abuses.

UAC, Holts, and Cadburys eventually concurred that a formal agreement was needed to curtail expenses and limit the bitter competition that had prevailed during the 1936-37 season. It was thought that the high cost of cocoa was mainly due to the large advances made to the buyers. Discussions centered on cutting allowances for mortgages and bonds, buying quotas, and elimination of the security system in which the farmer was required to give various types of security for monies advanced to him.

At an April 1937 meeting in Liverpool in which UAC and Holts participated, it was agreed that a short-term selling pool was needed for the Gold Coast, Nigerian, and Cameroon cocoa trade. Termination dates of August, September, and October 1937 were discussed.[13] Cadburys, however, did not join the discussions until June, by which time the marketing problems and trade abuses involving the expense of the advances system had become more pronounced. The problems with this system were a major concern to Holts, a comparative newcomer to the trade: During the summer two proposals were offered. The first was for a pool among the British cocoa-buying firms to control tonnage. The second was that the manufacturers agree among themselves to restrict tonnage and thus exempt themselves from a pool arrangement for buying. UAC objected to the second proposal because it doubted the effectiveness of such a scheme. Some of the manufacturing firms met in July to discuss the proposal arrangements and decided that there should be no limitation on future purchases. Cadburys representatives had stressed, at a June meeting with the merchandise firms, that their main concern was to guarantee their own supplies and to improve the quality of cocoa. They were determined not to undermine goodwill on the Coast, nor to be prevented from selling to other manufacturers. They concluded that if the prices paid to African producers were lowered, the government would be forced to act in order to protect the interests of the Africans. By mid-August, after further discussions, most of Cadburys concerns had been considered.[14]

During August almost all of the terms for the future agreement were worked out. The merchant firms, with the exception of the Co-operative Wholesale Society, agreed to join together to set a price for cocoa and to limit tonnage on the condition that the manufacturers join with them. It was decided that the price paid to the farmer would be based on the published market price, plus an allowance for expenses and a small profit. This price would not be compulsory, but the amount bought by each firm would be subject to a quota based on previous purchases.[15] Cadburys signed a private accord with the UAC for the purchase of cocoa from the company, should Cadburys be in short supply.

The agreement was to take effect in October and to last four years. There were insufficient signatures, however, and it was not implemented until November.[16] A subsidiary agreement gave the manufacturers the right to stop buying or to reduce their purchases below the agreed share after giving notice, and the right to call on the UAC for additional suppliers.

The Agreement and the Colonial Office

Immediately after an accord on the agreement had been reached, the firms sent letters of explanation to their Gold Coast agents.[17] Cadburys' letters were sent on September 18. Six days later, on September 24, Messrs. John Cadbury of Cadburys and Frank Samuel of UAC met with Colonial Office officials. At this meeting it was decided that the firms would send a statement explaining the agreement to the Secretary of State for the Colonies, W. G. A. Ormsby Gore (later Lord Harlech), and thereafter the Secretary of State would forward information about the proposal to the governors of the West African colonies with the suggestion that it be circulated in the field. The Secretary of State's communication was dated October 7.[18]

In their letters to the Colonial Office, Messrs. Cadbury and Samuel gave the following reasons for supporting the agreement. First was the high price of cocoa. Intense competition over a period of years and heavy expenses had resulted in prices higher on the Gold Coast than those on the world market. Second, commissions and allowances paid to brokers and other middlemen far exceeded the value of services rendered, and did nothing to benefit the actual producers. It was argued that the agreement would eliminate overpayments to intermediaries and assure a fair price for the producers.[19] Many Gold Coast farmers had until then realized little income from cocoa because of the small size of their holdings, rather than because of the price of cocoa. As a result many farmers were forced to borrow money and to mortage their farms. Both the uncurbed activities of brokers and the uncontrolled competition among the merchants, according to a justification written during the spring of 1938 by a Holts representative on the Coast, were factors operating to the disadvantage of the farmer.[20]

The members of the Agreement also requested that the Colonial Office send a representative to the London committee in order to satisfy the Government that African producers would receive a full and fair price.[21]

Messrs. Cadbury and Samuel emphasized throughout that the proposed agreement was concerned only with the purchase of cocoa and that each member retained complete freedom in selling. A committee representing the participating firms in London would determine quotas based on each firm's share of crop purchases in previous years. Should any firm purchase cocoa in excess of its quota, it would be obligated to resell the excess at a set price to those who had purchased less. The London committee would establish a standard price, but no member would be prohibited from paying a higher one. In September this price was estimated at 22*s* 6*d* per cwt.

A letter from the Colonial Office noted that copies of the firms' letter and description had been sent to the governors of the Gold Coast and Nigeria. It was also suggested that the firms issue for distribution on the Coast a short circular outlining the main points of the agreement. As noted above, the firms did issue various types of statements, first to their own agents. Finally, the letter stated that the Secretary of State for the colonies was consulting the governors of the respective territories about the appointment of an observer to the London committee.[22]

Since the Governor of the Gold Coast had been notified by the colonial secretary of the pending agreement, the firms, acting on the assumption that he would follow the suggestion from London to publicize the agreement, proceeded with their plans to put the agreement into effect. Yet the Governor of the Gold Coast did not, in fact, immediately send circulars about the agreement to the various field officials. The manager of the Cocoa Department of the UAC wrote his Gold Coast agent that

In the meantime, I think it is useful for you to know that the Government has been informed of the whole scheme and that there is certainly no opposition from that quarter. If this information is judiciously conveyed to interested Europeans, prominent Africans and influential buyers it may have some effect in counteracting the beliefs which exist in some quarters through misleading propaganda.[23]

One month after the Governor of the Gold Coast, Sir Arnold Hodson, had been informed, he sent a dispatch to the secretary of state for the colonies outlining his and his advisers, objections to the agreement:

(i) The existence of a Buying Agreement in respect of Gold Coast Cocoa, which constitutes such a large proportion of the total world output must, in their opinion, have a depressing effect on world market prices; (ii) a deliberate suppression of local competition was bound to remove influences which had tended in the past to raise prices locally to the advantage of farmers; and (iii) the economic fairness of the Agreement apart; its continuance was certain, in the existing circumstances, to embitter the relations between Europeans and Africans and disorganize trade.[24]

Following the 1935-36 season "when a normal price may be said to have prevailed, middlemen advanced for the 1936-37 crop prices between 6/- and 10/- [shillings] a load of 60 pounds."[25] During that season the actual price to the farmer rose to over £1 per load. When the agreement was announced in the last part of September 1937, the price was expected to decline, because American buying, which had sustained it until then, was tapering off and the new crop was reported to be a good one. The price of cocoa in Accra at the end of September was between 35 and 40 shillings per cwt. (cwt. is 112 lbs, or 1/20 th of a long ton; thus the price per load was 26 shillings). By late

October the price to the farmer remained around 27 shillings.[26]

Competition among the firms in an overtraded area during 1937 had caused them to urge middlemen and brokers to secure as much tonnage as possible, which led to overdeclarations, cash advances, and high commissions and allowances. Under the circumstances, as the prices fell, the brokers would be sustaining a loss, because the price of the 1937-38 crop was considerably less than the advance of approximately 14 to 15 shillings paid (the price before transport charges were added). Hence the brokers had a good reason for advocating a hold-up. In this they were supported by the chiefs.

An announcement of the agreement appeared in the Gold Coast newspapers simultaneously with a fall in the world price for cocoa. By November 1, 1937, the Gold Coast farmers, and soon after the Ashanti farmers, began a hold-up of cocoa and a boycott, which were so effective, according to the letter of presentation accompanying the Report of the Commission on the Marketing of West African Cocoa (Cmd. 5845), "as to bring both the export and the internal trade in the Gold Coast practically to a stand-still, only small quantities of cocoa were marketed, and imported merchandise accumulated unsold in the firms' stores and in the Customs sheds".[27]

The Cocoa Hold-Up

During the latter part of 1937, representatives of the firms made frequent contacts with the Colonial Office in London and with government officials on the Gold Coast.[28] Mr. Cadbury left for the Gold Coast when it was apparent that there was strong opposition to the Agreement. Once there, he realized that 'all Africans were very suspicious of the Scheme" and that they linked the fall in prices to the agreement. He had an interview with the Colonial Secretary on October 23, the first in two months of meetings with officials, agents of other firms, and the Gold Coast chiefs and farmers in Accra, Kumasi, and other areas. A month later Frank Samuel of the UAC joined him. During this period contacts with the government in London, especially with the Office of the Secretary of State for the Colonies, were made by individual firms involved in the buying of cocoa rather than by the Joint West Africa Committee.[29] Relations between the firms and the government in London appeared good.

During the first part of November Mr Cadbury met with Nana Sir Ofori Atta, the Okyenhene of Akim Abuakwa (a paramount chief from the eastern Province), and with a member of the Legislative Council. On November 5 the *Echo* wrote that Mr. Cadbury spoke "with carefulness and tact", He was quoted as saying "bluntly that the pool would benefit everybody", unlike the previous year, when prices were higher than the market demanded and "led to speculation". Nana Sir Ofori Atta expressed his "great surprise that Cadburys who always followed the grand tradition of a great ideal should have connected themselves with a movement which is viewed in this country with gravest disfavour". In an editorial on November 25, the *Echo,* referring to a conference of farmers and merchants held at the Legislative Council Chamber, commented that "the more we tell of the position which Mr. Cadbury holds . . . the more the farmers are amazed at the utterance of the representatives of one of the firms which formerly the farmers were proud to call their friends".

In his discussions with farmers and chiefs, Mr. Cadbury argued that his firm could not continue in business in the Gold Coast if the price of cocoa were cheaper at home than on the Coast.[30] Cadburys, he stated, had entered the agreement to assure a fair price for both producers and buyers, to proteot the buying organizations of smaller firms and to see that other concerns, including the UAC, would give a fair price. He pointed out that the opening price of the 1937 season, barely in excess of 10*s* per load, had been ignored, while the highest price of the season, 20*s* per head load of 60 pounds, was recalled.[31]

When Mr. Samuel of UAC arrived in the Gold Coast at the end of November, it was evident that there was considerable animosity toward his firm. In part this was because the UAC was one of the largest firms there. In addition, as it had been formed from a merger of concerns which had been important in Coast trade since the beginning of the century, criticisms of these earlier companies, just or not, were carried over and directed at the UAC. Mr. Samuel joined Mr. Cadbury in his efforts to reach some accord with the producers, and both men made suggestions to the London Committee and kept it informed. Also, with the assistance of Messrs. Edwards of Cadburys, FitzGerald of UAC, and Ellis and Hood of Cadburys, they prepared a statement that was presented to the chiefs and farmers at Kumasi on December 7.[32]

In the speech Mr. Samuel explained the UAC position. He regretted any misunderstanding but maintained that the agreement was necessary and that the producers would receive full market value for their cocoa.

What do you mean by this? We mean the highest price at which you can sell your cocoa in any country in the world. There is no secret about this price. It is published every day in the newspapers in London, Hamburg and New York.

You of course understand that the actual costs of buying . . . have to be deducted from the world's market price.[33]

Accordingly the firms had presented to the Governor a list of expenses to be deducted. Mr Samuel stated that there was nothing in the agreement to prevent a firm from paying a higher price than the world price, "but if as a result he buys more cocoa than his agreed share, he must sell the extra quantity to those who have bought less than their share". If a firm did not pay the full world price, large firms like American Hershey would quickly realize their advantage and come to Ashanti to buy directly. He also explained the quota system and a little known provision that would prevent merchants from enticing buyers working for one firm to leave for another. During the subsequent discussion Mr. Samuel urged the appointment of a mediator, and proposed to consult with his "principals in England" about finding someone mutually acceptable.

As the hold-up continued into 1938, cocoa was burned in the Nsawam area. The chiefs and farmers met in Accra, where they reaffirmed their opposition to the "Pool." In Kumasi the cocoa trade remained at a standstill, although other trade increased.[34]

According to an unofficial UAC historian, the agreement among the firms had caused concern only in the Gold Coast. He described the situation as follows: "An agreement by the firms to pool their purchases almost synchronized with a fall in the world value of the commodity. The farmers attributed the drop in price to the former instead of the latter event, and the hold-up of supplies was the method which they adopted of protesting against the pool."[35]

Despite the efforts of the firms to counteract adverse publicity about the agreement, the hold-up continued. The UAC author raised the question of whether it was the farmers who attributed low prices to the agreement, or whether they were dominated by a small group of "irreconcilables". Another possible reason for the hold-up was the fear of monopoly. Even producers who did not object to the attempt to keep current prices close to world market prices feared that the agreement would enable the firms to take advantage of them in the future. The UAC historian stated that

In the course of the controversy reference was made to the monopoly once wielded by the Royal Niger Company. The Charter granted to the Royal Niger Company expressly prohibited it from monopolizing trade but conferred upon it large powers of government and the right to levy customs duties, provided the revenue from them was exclusively devoted to defraying the cost of government. The Royal Niger Company nevertheless did succeed in virtually monopolizing trade in the region under its jurisdiction without infringing the letter of the Charter. The action has been defended on the ground that it could not have carried out its government functions nearly as efficiently as it did . . . had it not kept practical control of trade.[36]

The Niger Company reported a profit of from 6 to 7 percent, which did not seem excessive to the UAC author, who concluded:

The Firms do not co-operate to make exorbitant the rates of profit. They will know it to be impossible. What they seek is to stabilize trade and create such conditions as will enable them to obtain a modest but fairly steady return on their capital. It would not be in the interests of the country that trade should cease to attract capital by becoming chronically unremunerative.[37]

Neither the firms' representatives nor the Colonial officials in London or on the Coast realized that the farmers would be able to organize a boycott so successfully. A district officer reporting to the Chief Commissioner for Kumasi stated that:

Although most of the chiefs were themselves wealthy cocoa farmers and able to stand the financial strain of a hold-up, they were not in a position to impose such conditions on their people against their will; had they tried to do so they would have risked destoolment.[38] On the contrary, they were tailing along behind the majority will, and when they gave an order to stop selling they were the mouth-piece of majority opinion. Not surprisingly there were some farmers not in accord with the stoppage of selling and these were ready enough to tell the firms that it was not their fault that they could not sell . . .[39]

Press Reception

The English press published news of the agreement during September, and by October rumors had reached the Gold Coast, where reports were highly critical. Some excerpts from the English and Gold Coast press will illustrate the differing receptions accorded the agreement and the conditions under which the firms were to meet in efforts to clarify the agreement and settle the hold-up. The *Evening Standard* and the *Daily Express* were among the first to publish reports of the agreement. On September 14 the *Evening Standard* wrote that there were twelve West African shippers involved, of which the UAC was the most important. The agreement was attributed to the desire of the manufacturers to prevent the big shippers from monopolizing the trade, and was described as a necessary reaction to competition as "prices have been forced well above the terminal market level and consequently trade has often been uneconomic". It also mentioned that the agreement was not a pool arrangement, and it was expected that the New York market would regard it with suspicion. The *Daily Express* on the same date inaccurately reported that the new arrangement would include shippers from the United States. It did point out that the agreement would benefit the big groups on the West Coast, thereby reducing the expenses of their buying organizations. It also publicized the firms' contention that the agreement would stabilize the market, which had fluctuated widely during the previous year. On September 15 both the *News Chronicle* and the *Financial Times* expressed the hope that the proposed agreement would abolish abuses, such as undue advances to native brokers, and that it would systematize the method whereby prices on the West Coast were kept in touch with quotas on the Liverpool market. It was noted that there was no intention to form a pool, and that interest groups in the United States were not parties to the arrangement as "suggested in some quarters. While the biggest cocoa terminal market in the world is New York, United States consumers do not buy directly from the Gold Coast. All their purchases are made either through this country or the Continent".

The *Financial Times* on October 1 reported that the agreement would limit price fluctuations and improve crop reporting techniques. It noted that a record new crop was expected during the 1937-38 season but that during the last few months the actual

consumption of retained cocoa imports had been disappointing. The
correspondent estimated that the New York quotations would drop
and that a price of about 30s per hundred weight could not be
regarded as high.

In West Africa both public opinion and the press connected the
decline in cocoa prices with the agreement, [40] particularly since news
of both had arrived at about the same time. *West Africa* mentioned
the agreement on September 18, but the periodical probably did not
circulate in the Gold Coast until later.[41] On the same date the *Gold
Coast Independent* printed an article about the opening of the cocoa
season, and in a bold print subtitle wrote "Price Manipulators Busy."
This article, however, showed no knowledge of an agreement, but
indicated in general terms that the farmers

are actually robbed by sharp practices on the part of those who interest it is
that these horny sons of toil get the maximum returns from their labours—
the Merchants. . . . The farmers patronize the stores of the trading
establishments, yet these trading houses have no scruples in manipulating the
prices by which the buying capacity of their best customers is restricted.

In the September 1937 issue of the *Independent,* "Digit" implied some
knowledge of the agreement, yet made no specific reference to it;
rather, under the headings "Tampering with Prices" and "New
Arrivals", he stated that the "news of the attempt being made at this
early stage of the season to tamper with the price of cocoa has not
made good reading". He noted that the "old stagers" had lost control
during tne previous season, resulting in the farmer getting back a bit
of his own, because the new arrivals in the cocoa trade had not been
"shepherded into the tricks of the trade before the cocoa season
broke upon them". The *African Morning Post* reported on September
30 that "The Pool commences operations from tomorrow. Since the
Pool was formed the cocoa price has dropped nearly £10 per ton".
The *Post* considered 20s a load to be a fair price, urged the farmers to
refrain from selling "until you get 20s", and concluded that
"Perhaps Government when they see they are losing about £300,000
through the actives [another term for "broker"] of the Pool, they will
take action against the Trusts".[42]

Anokwalefo wrote in the *African Morning Post* on October 5 that
there was a general outcry against the pool and asserted that the
brokers and factors "are the arch-enemies of the farmers . . . That
whatever may be the case against the Pool the European is not soley
to blame. When he sees that we are up for our rights, he steps back a
little. It is our own kith and kin—the brokers and factors that do the
tricks". The *Post* continued its articles about the agreement and on
October 7 printed an article by Osampa which stressed the need for
the African to educate himself and make sacrifices so as to overcome
European control.

On October 7 *The Echo* published a long article that reported meetings of some large farmers' groups and their plans to resist the agreement. In what was known as "The London Letter", *The Echo* described the agreement, which it stated would be signed within the next few days by twelve West African shippers and which would end some abuses in cocoa trade. Then under the heading "No Pool", the city editor commented that "Though the document does not subscribe any view to the assumption that a pool has been formed, the very agreement is in this spirit otherwise it has no meaning in fact and is utterly worthless. We are certain that the United States is in no way connected . . .".

The Commission of Enquiry

On December 14, 1937 after frequent communications between the representatives in Accra and members of the London Committee— including at times Messrs. George Cadbury of Cadburys and Jasper Knight, A. R. I. Mellor, and Lord Trenchard of UAC—a declaration was issued. The firms announced their intention of enforcing the agreement and their readiness to buy cocoa at a fair market price.

The London Committee reported that its relations with the Colonial Office were "extremely satisfactory", while the firms' representatives in the Gold Coast reported that the Governor's opposition to the formation of the agreement seemingly had not changed by December.[43] Messrs. Cadbury and Samuel also told the London Committee that they viewed the hold-up as a spontaneous movement, expressing the determination of the Gold Coast people not to tolerate a buying agreement, and that the chiefs were merely interpreting the wishes of their people.[44] The firms, in general, including UAC and Cadburys, concluded that the hold-up was the result of agitation by a small group and that it was encouraged by the press. The Governor requested that the firms scrap the agreement, but the representatives of the firms thought that this would not lead to a resumption of normal trading because of the continued low prices, the general unrest in the country, and the possibility of provincial councils interpreting such actions differently. Neither did the firms agree with the Governor that serious disturbances would ensue if the Agreement remained in force. As the hold-up continued, the representatives reported that "Despite complete cessation of cocoa sales and virtual stoppage of trading there are no surface signs of bad feeling among the masses although there have been isolated cases of hooliganism".[45]

The Secretary of State urged publication of the agreement and offered to publish it in the *Gazette*. The London Committee concurred on the condition that its representatives in Accra give consent. The latter, however, were strongly opposed on the grounds that the press would probably misrepresent the agreement and that "more trouble could be caused by publication at this late date", as a great deal of explanatory material would be needed and some would consider this material was not binding and thus not acceptable.[46] The Governor supported publication, although he thought it would be of little help. On the basis of the reports from Accra, the London Committee decided against publication and informed the Colonial Office of its decision to issue the declaration and informed the Colonial Office of its decision to issue the declaration instead.[47]

In response to the situation, the governors of the Gold Coast and Nigeria now recommended the establishment of a commission of enquiry to investigate the marketing of cocoa.[48] The Commission was announced in the British Parliament on February 14, 1938.

The London Committee continued its meetings, and appointed a subcommittee composed of Messrs. John Cadbury, Frank Samuel, and John Holt of Holts to present its case to the Commission of Enquiry in London. Testimony was first presented in Accra to the Commission by the firms' representatives, some of whom were sent from England. UAC sent Mr. A. R. I. Mellor, and Cadburys' Mr. N. Edwards to help prepare the firms' testimony.[49] The London Committee requested that all agents on the Coast cooperate with Messrs. Mellor and Edwards in presenting evidence to the Commission, and that they accept their advice as far as possible. In the case of disagreement, they were instructed to cable the head office. Holts sent Mr. R. E. Beard to represent them while the Commission was sitting on the Coast in April, and to represent the company in all conversations with Messrs. Mellor and Edwards. The subcommittee on the Coast stated, in its communication to the firms' agents there, that much of the evidence which the companies would like to give was political in nature and should not be submitted, since a commission of this sort should deal in facts which could be upheld under cross examination.[50] The main agents of the firms on the Coast, which ascribed to the agreement, ultimately gave individual testimonies, for they did not always agree with the firms' London representatives.

During March there were no cocoa sales in Accra, although farmers in Hohoe continued to trade. In some official circles, according to a report from a Holt agent on the Coast, it was thought that the Hold-Up had been instigated by the chiefs, who maintained it by intimidating the farmers.[51] Such allegations about the role of the chiefs were alluded to in the firms' testimonies. One example cited was that the Confederacy Council, composed of chiefs, in a meeting on March 10 suggested that farmers who continued to sell cocoa be brought before the Assembly.[52] Nana Sir Ofori Atta had been quoted in the *Gold Coast News* on November 19, 1937, however, as saying that no chief would dream of ordering a farmer not to sell his cocoa. Also the chief commissioner of Ashanti, at the end of April 1938, declared his conviction that the hold-up in Ashanti had started from the bottom, not from the top.[53] On April 14, while the Commission was taking testimony, the chiefs again met in Accra and elected to continue the hold-up because prices were still low.[54]

As the hearings in the Gold Coast neared their end, Mr. Mellor reported that representatives of the firms were in touch with the Governor in Accra and the Colonial Office in London. Some Commission members implied suspicions about Mellor aiding with preparation of the firms' testimonies, but Mellor indicated that he ignored these slighting references. (As noted above, besides testimony from Mr. Mellor, a number of the firms' agents also presented their own testimony.) Mellor further stated that his instructions were to sign a declaration suspending the agreement until October 1 if the chiefs and farmers would sign a statement undertaking certain guarantees regarding the supply of cocoa. Since legislation had just been passed to regulate the export of cocoa, the firms were willing to do this.[55]

Attention also centered on the boycott. A representative of Holts brought out the point that a high market price, "and therefore a correspondingly high price here is particularly welcome to an organization" that bought produce and sold merchandise. It was obvious, this representative stated, that the "greater the sum of money put into circulation by our payments for cocoa the larger will be our sales of goods—this latter being our main objective in being here at all."[56]

In an article in the *Manchester Guardian*, the financial editor doubted that West African consumers would either rapidly or fully regain their spending power. British exports of cotton goods had declined during the first quarter by more than three quarters compared with the same period the previous year. Since the cocoa Hold-Up had been supplemented by a buyers' boycott of imported goods, he expected that part of the trade would be regained, and summarized market conditions as follows:

In spite of the fact that cocoa shipments from the colonies (which supplies normally about 45 percent of the world's cocoa) totalled only 49,365 metric tons in the first six months of the current season (October to March), compared with 216,100 tons in the corresponding period of the last year, the London price for Accra cocoa declined about 20 percent between October 1, 1937, and the announcement of the lifting of the boycott on April 13. Since then the decline has been accelerated and the London July quotation for Accra cocoa now fluctuates between 20*s* and 21*s* 6*d* per hundredweight, compared with over 30*s* on October 1 and nearly 60*s* at the beginning of 1937. The producers have scant hopes of getting better terms during the rest of the 1937-38 cocoa season, which ends in September 30. The current demand for cocoa is small. Actual consumption is on the decline (current trade estimates predict a decline in world consumption of 10 to 20 percent this season), while the resumption of the Gold Coast sales coincides with the sale of the current Brazilian crop.[57]

It was expected that Gold Coast cocoa sales during the 1937-38 season would reach 200,000 tons at 25*s* per hundredweight, as compared with 305,000 metric tons at the average price of over 35*s* per hundredweight in the previous season. The article pointed out that the temporary export licensing system currently provided very large quotas, but that they would lapse in October; hence it would be difficult for a reform of marketing methods to raise the international price for cocoa, "which, as the Colonial Secretary has stated, is determined not by the Gold Coast shippers (among whom the Gold Coast boycott was directed) but by the New York market. Only international action can improve the outlook".[58]

The firms indicated, in the evidence they presented before the Commission in London, displeasure with the government's publication of information on the agreement. Frank Samuel and John Cadbury presented evidence together which disputed the neutrality of the government.

In any case we contend that the attitude which the Government described as neutrality was in fact no such thing. The firms had submitted their scheme to the Government. If it had been objectionable, there is not the slightest doubt that the Government would have so declared and even taken steps to frustrate it, yet when the reverse was the case impartiality never impelled them to any declaration. The people were not slow to interpret this sort of neutrality as condemnation of the scheme. Nor did the Government even enforce law and give protection to those who desired to market.[59]

They interpreted the administration's neutrality as condemnation of the firms and not support as suggested by Wolfson. They submitted further that the administration in the Colony and in Ashanti, by insisting that the people would pay no attention to information issued by them, had in fact indicated that they lacked real influence over the people. The administration thus implied that the people "regard their Chiefs and their Chiefs alone, as the authority to whom they must turn, and from whose word there is no effective appeal". Samuel and Cadbury then said that even if this were true, "it surely does not constitute a sound reason for abandoning all attempt to give wise counsel" to the people. The failure of the Gold Coast government to give information about the agreement had thus contributed to the crises of 1937-38.[60]

Mr. Jasper Knight presented the UAC position to the Commission in London. He concentrated on the large investment of UAC in the trade and the company's overhead expenses, strictly attributable to cocoa, which amounted to around £100,000. In addition, he noted that competition between the firms for the trade had become stronger, and that the manufacturers had increased the percentage of the crop which they bought. Cadbury's share had accordingly increased by 16 percent in the 1936-37 season. Such increases in the competition made it necessary for UAC to find a way to maintain its investment on the Coast. Mr. Knight then proposed a cocoa marketing company.[61]

The manufacturing companies also testified to their commitment in the West African trade.[62] The chief source of loss in the trade was, according to this evidence, payments to African brokers, and the agreement was designed to correct these abuses. The firms declared their policy to be "Fair treatment of the producers". Illustrations of assistance in education, training, and employment were also offered in the evidence.

At a meeting of Lever Brothers and Unilever in May 1938, the chairman reported a loss of £1,000,000 by the UAC and denied the accusation that the UAC and other merchant firms had deliberately brought about the fall in prices. In the final report of the Commission, mention was made of the fact that the UAC, the largest shipper with half the trade, was viewed by the African witnesses with "fear and suspicion because of the concentration of business in the hands of this one large concern".[63]

The findings of the Commission was made public in Accra on October 24, 1938. Its main recommendations dealt with the withdrawal of the agreement and the establishment of statutory marketing boards. The report also deplored the haste with which the agreement had been introduced. According to one source, it was difficult to obtain an opinion from producers and chiefs about the report, because they were "rather puzzled" by it. The local press expressed disappointment that the Commission had been unable to secure a higher standard price for cocoa.[64]

The firms considered reactivating the agreement but decided against it for fear of more trouble.[65] A suggestion to set up a pool in England only was also vetoed, on the grounds that the prices would still fluctuate from day to day and that each firm would retain its own buying system.[66] The firms now viewed the problem as primarily political, and felt that they should show no antagonism toward the Commission Report, as both colonial officials and Africans were "intensely suspicious of the merchants" and could be expected to oppose anything they favored.

The Gold Coast government set up two committees—one in Accra and the other in Kumasi—to study the report and make recommendations about its implementation. As the Accra committee was to formulate a merchandising plan, the former members of the pool voted in January 1939 to send a representative to its deliberations.[67] The committees continued to meet into April. Progress was delayed because the various groups were unable to agree, and each item of the report was thoroughly discussed. The producers opposed any plan that would make the marketing of cocoa compulsory or that would give the chiefs any control over the marketing of cocoa.[68] In this connection it was asserted that Nana Sir Ofori Atta would support a compulsory marketing scheme in order to increase his own tonnage allotment and obtain further control over the merchandise trade. While the farmers continued to support the retention of their independence in marketing, the firms worked for some kind of regulation. It was not until the late spring of 1939 that draft schemes were presented by the committees. The Accra Committee essentially supported the collective marketing scheme and suggested implementation procedures for certain recommendations of the Commission. The Kumasi report, which was quite long, included much detail about possible operational problems.[69] Before any action could be taken on these proposals, wartime controls were instituted.

Conclusions

The firms. The cocoa Hold-Up of 1937-38 was one of several occurring on the West Coast during the twentieth century. The 1930-31 Hold-Up arose from farmers' objections to a trading agreement being formed by the firms buying cocoa. The 1937-38 Hold-Up, which occurred for similar reasons, brought to light elements of the existing economic and political situation and emphasized the active role that farmers and other members of the West African community might play.

For a trade such as cocoa in Ghana, it is difficult to obtain detailed financial records for firms and then to evaluate, over a period of years, the profits and losses, though of course the various companies dealing in the West African cocoa trade certainly continued to evaluate these aspects of their operations, particularly as the price of cocoa declined, first in the United States, and then on the London market. UAC indicated that in 1937 they were losing about £1 million per year.[70] Although questions can be raised about the accounting procedures which lead to such conclusions, it seems likely that their estimates of loses for the period were reasonably accurate. However, the company was sufficiently diversified to be able to cover these losses.

The price to the farmer for cocoa during this period was reduced, on the basis of the United States price, from approximately £30 in the 1936-37 season to £14 in the 1937-38 season.[71] The agreement, it should be remembered, was to establish quotas for each firm, not to fix prices of cocoa.

The Colonial Office. During the 1930's business-initiated contacts with colonial officials in London and on the Coast were limited to discussions on specific issues. There was no arrangement for regular meetings, nor did the colonial administration seem to seek advice from the firms, although good relationships existed between them when the firms representatives discussed particular problems with the respective officials. Despite the recommendations of a colonial secretary, there were no regular meetings between the West Africa Committee and the Colonial Office.[72] During World II it was again the business firms which initiated contact and suggested wartime marketing controls. At no time did the Colonial Office solicit the assistance of business or ask for their views on development plans for the colony.

Typical of government's attitude toward business before World War II was the distrust of the firms displayed by the Colonial Administration. Historically this attitude was prevalent in the Colonial Services and may have resulted from a difference in background and education between the groups, specifically in the study of business.[73] The Service, in general, was little concerned with economic affairs and then only when problems were brought forth. The Colonial Office did not establish an economic section until the 1930's and then it was staffed by only two people.

The Coast administration shared the farmers' suspicion of the agreement and maintained that the agreement would put the firms in a position to take advantage of the farmers. In this they followed the reasoning of some chiefs and leaders of the Hold-Up. It could be argued that the Colonial Administration on the Coast took a paternalistic view toward the farmers and, by expressing opposition to the spread of information about the agreement, was attempting to protect them.

The Governor's failure to circulate immediately information about the agreement can be viewed also as an attempt to protect the farmers. The Colonial Office was unaware of the Gold Coast government's attitudes toward the agreement until the Governor's communication was received over a month later.

The failure of the Coast administration to publicize the agreement immediately, as London had instructed, led to misunderstanding on the part of the farmers and the chiefs and created suspicious attitudes toward the firms. Some firms that signed the agreement had already been viewed with suspicion, while others, such as Cadburys, were not suspected until revelations about the agreement were circulated.

The failure to publicize the agreement also reflects a lack of coordination between the Colonial Office in London and the administration in the field, which was characteristic of the Colonial Service before the Second World War. Air mail service at the time of the Hold-Up had only just been introduced. Prior to this, communications between London and overseas personnel were so slow that colonial officers customarily took action on their own initiative. In this regard the firms probably should have taken into account the traditionally accepted independence of the Colonial

Administration, and therefore should not have automatically assumed that information about the agreement had been disseminated.

During the 1930's the Coast administration moved from a position of regarding business interests as a threat to the local population to a position of more willingness to work with business in local affairs. Businessmen came to be represented in the legislative council that advised the Governor. Personnel of the firms who were of long residence participated in social affairs. Even so, the Governor of the Gold Coast viewed business with sufficient distrust to block efforts to enforce the agreement.

Indications of future political tension on the Coast became manifest during the Cocoa Crisis of 1937-38. The Coast farmers, with only spasmodic organizational experience, demonstrated a cohesiveness that was felt in economic and governmental affairs,[74] and business laid the foundation for later marketing arrangements in cooperation with government boards. It was not until long after World War II, however, that cooperation in economic affairs developed between business and government. A. G. Hopkins characterized this pre-war period as the beginning of the radical movement supporting a system of complete political and economic independence.[75]

The firms, through London, laid the foundation for future cocoa marketing arrangements, which resulted finally not in private agreements between the firms, but rather in cooperative efforts with the governmental boards. It was from the relationships established during the Hold-Up that trends toward more permanent patterns of cooperation between business and government were begun. Relations with the inhabitants of the colony also change. During World War II some programs for local control were instituted. It was not until after the disturbances of 1948, however, that the local administrators relinquished paternalism and protectionism and encouraged local participation in governmental affairs. The basis for the post-war independence movement was previewed in the boycott organization of the farmers during the 1937-38 crisis.

The Firms' Contribution to Development 1937-39. The merchant and manufacturing firms buying cocoa on the Coast in 1937 and 1938 indicated, through their testimony to the Commission on West African Cocoa Marketing, that their concern was with maintaining their investment in West Africa. The manufacturing firms also gave evidence indicating that the producer should be considered, stating that the signatories to the agreement had considered the interest of the producer and the welfare of the Coastal people. Collating the firms' activities on the Coast in 1937-38 with the categories describing businesses in the development process (mentioned in the introduction), we consider as innovative activities of the firms which involve the interests of the producer and the welfare of the Coastal people. Certainly the testimony of the firms clearly pointed to the common interest of the buying firms and the producer, as opposed to the middleman and the broker. By 1937-38 Cadburys had contributed for over ten years to the establishment of Achimota College, and had begun to employ Africans in the firm's business. UAC during the last part of the thirties brought a few Africans into management-training program (see Chapter 6 for details). The employment and training of the Ghanaians by the firms demonstrated that the firms' economic concerns and the welfare of the people could coincide.

The economic concerns of the firms could be categorized in part as exploitation when considering the exportation of cocoa and other commodities for refinement and for manufacture. Yet during the depression in prices of 1937-38 firms continued to buy cocoa in what was considered by them, especially UAC and Holts, to be a cutthroat market situation and profitless trade. UAC was able to cover its losses during this season only through other of its diversified activities.

Finally, Cadburys' evident concern and involvement in efforts to improve the quality of cocoa through frequent representations to the government involved mixed motivations of profit-making and general improvemnet of the farmers' conditions.[76] Thus exploitative and innovative elements were mixed in the same action.

3

WARTIME CONTROLS AND COCOA MARKETING

The Commission Report on the Hold-Up was still not implemented by the beginning of World War II. When the war began, the British government, partly at the urging of British business, decided to set up controls for the marketing of produce from various parts of the Empire. Such controls seemed essential to protect the livelihood of areas whose existence largely depended on the marketing of products not essential to the war effort.[1] West Africa, with its cocoa crop, was just such an area. In addition, large buyers expressed concern about being left with luxury items. Some form of government price assurance was necessary. This chapter focuses on the favorable reception by British business firms of wartime controls, and their very active part in implementing these controls.

A. G. Hopkins has suggested that since the turn of the century there have been three stages of economic development in the Gold Coast.[2] Before World War I economic issues arose only occasionally, and there was no economic policy. In the second stage a local figure, Tete-Ansa, attempted to establish, through a program of moderate reform, a banking and business complex to face some of the economic problems that had surfaced. With the failure of the program in the mïd-1930's, according to Hopkins, the radical movement came into being, and was directed toward complete political and economic independence. The Cocoa Hold-Up of 1938 reflected some of the dissatisfactions of the people on the Coast, but it remained for the events of the Second World War and the postwar period to bring controls for the marketing and supply of goods. These controls, though different from either alternative postulated in 1939, delayed the further demonstration of the people's dissatisfactions.

As Great Britain entered upon wartime activities, the Gold Coast also became involved in the World War.[3] West Africa was already a part of the economic and political system of Britain and realized this connection more intimately as London began to apply governmental controls over various aspects of the economy in all the British territories. For the first time since Britain had asserted control over

31

West Africa, the Administration appealed to the people of the area to support the war effort as members of the British Empire.[4]

The Controls

Controls on the export and purchase of merchandise and foods in West Africa were first handled in London by the Ministry of Food. In the issues November 9 and December 12, 1939, of the *Gold Coast Gazette* the Defense Regulations for government purchase and sale of cocoa appeared. A. C. Miles, Acting Director of Agriculture, made the announcement. Controls, including licensing of shippers and allotment of shipping space, were also established for the shipment of other produce, such as cocoa butter. Some additional regulations were written into the Emergency Power Defense Act of 1939, including subsection 1 of Section 1 concerning Control of Merchandise and a Central Price Regulation Advisory Committee. Controlled produce sales included—in addition to cocoa—bananas, palm kernels, fruits, and copra.[5]

Before their enactment, both groups of regulations were circulated and discussed with various business firms. The records of Holts for the period include lengthy discussions about the operations of these controls of cocoa and frequently supported no fixed control price.[6] Discussion about regulations on oleaginous products appeared in the November records:

1. A primary function of the Ministry of Food would appear to be to prevent an uncontrolled rise in the cost of living in this country [England]. In the same way the French Ministry of Food will try to implement that responsibility in France. The argument behind the economic plan appears to be something like this. In 1918 the war was costing us in this country seven million pounds per day. Inflation, largely uncontrolled . . . had been allowed to occur between 1914 and 1918 with a consequence that, at the end of the war, the pre-war £ was worth 10/-in terms of real wages and real investment returns. We ended the war with a terrific war debt and an inflated currency . . .

2. This highly mechanised war, if and when it really gets going, will probably cost per day very much more than the last one did. If the war lasts for a long time, we shall probably end with a war debt which, if it is allowed to be increased by preventable inflation would be of such a magnitude that it will bring untold misery from deflation or a permanent debt . . . The view appears to be that anything is better than either of those alternatives and that any increase in prices above prewar must be grimly fought unless and until it is impossible to get what supplies are wanted without some further inflation.[7]

Ways to involve the African farmer in more production were discussed along with efforts to enforce controls. At least five related points were raised in the Holts memorandum:

3. . . . The argument is that, once a peasant has produced enough money crop to pay his taxes and to provide him with his small comforts and luxuries, he has no further incentive to prevent it [inflation].

4. The argument is based on the assumption that if Nigeria will produce double its 1938 exports of oleaginous produce, the Allied Governments will be glad to have it and that shipping will be made available to carry it. . . .

6. Admittedly, the selling prices of imports in West Africa have risen owing to increased first costs, war risk insurance and freights, but the oleaginous farmer has the advantage, not possessed by other sections of the community, that the return to him of his money crop can be increased with his own will because he can produce more.

7. Increased production can come about in two ways. Firstly, each farmer's own land can produce a little more. But, secondly, the main increase in volume must come from the utilization of resources not at present exporting. Low prices below a certain point must mean low export volume because there is a definite limitation of the radius from the port within which transport costs of the port are supportable. The important thing is to try to do something to iron out the inequalities brought about by geographical fortuity. . . .

8. The African peasant should not be encouraged to believe that only when the Empire is at war does he get large prices for his produce. He should be reminded that this war is as much his war as ours, and that he knows full well what will happen to him if we lose it. He is being asked to make his contribution by doing more work but with the difference that, in his case, he is going to be paid extra for that work.[8]

The Food Control Office in Nigeria stated in a November meeting that volunteer rationing of certain products, such as butter, should be continued mainly because these products had not become an important part of the West African diet.[9]

Administrative Arrangements for Wartime Controls.[10] With the outbreak of war the cocoa-purchasing firms became concerned about the shipping of such luxury items as cocoa and the marketing of the crop. Mr. John Cadbury took the problem to the government in London.[11] Soon he was involved in plans for produce control and became Director of the West African Cocoa Control Board established in late 1939 under the Ministry of Food. The Ministry assumed control over the marketing of cocoa, since the Colonial Office had neither facilities nor powers for trading and thus no power to buy produce. Mr. (now Sir Eric) Tansley, who soon joined Mr. Cadbury as Marketing Director and then went with the Board (later in 1940 the West African Produce Control Board) to the Colonial Office, made arrangements and allotments for shipping space assigned to the Board by the Ministry of War Transport, the office with ultimate responsibility for all shipping space.[12]

The Association of West African Merchants (AWAM) provided price consultation in London. On the Coast, representatives of the firms in AWAM served the government as advisory agents on the selling of cocoa. Cadburys decided to join AWAM in 1939 and remained in the Association through 1947.[13] The Cocoa Sub-Committee of AWAM served, during the war, as liaison with the West African Produce Control Board.[14]

Shippers on the Coast were divided into groups. Group A included concerns that had already shipped cocoa under the temporary licensing procedures of July 1938.[15] These shippers continued with a renewal of licenses. Group B shippers could apply for licenses to sell.[16] The Buying Agreement was suspended in April 1938, after the Hold-Up, and was not revived. Suspension was discussed and approved by the firms at intervals until the War in 1939.[17]

The manager of Holts explained the arrangements in a communication to Accra and Lagos:

1.   NOMINATION
     Group B Agents are being nominated by Group B Shippers to act as their Agents under the Control Scheme, subject to the approval of the Central Control. The official nominations will be those cabled by the Governors.

2.   AGREEMENT
     A short agreement between the Central Control and the Group B Agents is being prepared and will be submitted to the Agents as soon as possible. The agreement will cover the period of the scheme up to the end of September 1940. During this period Group B shippers have the right to cease selling through the Group B Agents.

3.   Meanwhile, so that trade can continue with the least possibility of misunderstanding, the Central Control wish the Group B Agents to make a careful note of the following:
     Tonnage Quota . . .
     Buying Price . . .
     Bags . . .
     Lighterage . . .
     Settlement . . .
     Commission . . .
     Correspondence . . .

4.   These prices will hold firm throughout the season without change. We understand the Ministry of Food will own the cocoa though they will only pay us at the end of the season and we will do the finance. It will be sold under their directions and at their risk. If in the event it should prove that they can get good prices from neutral countries, then they will make the profit on behalf of the British taxpayer, who will apparently stand the loss if there is a loss.

5.   There will thus be no local speculation because there will be no market fluctuation. There are a good many details yet to work out and Mr John [Cadbury] is at the moment in London engaged in that. In practice at all events, the cocoa agreement will remain, though it is not too clear yet if it will be possible to work the pool without actual physical hand-overs. Further instructions about all that will follow.

6. To give you an indication as to how serious the position was, it was, until recently, quite problematical whether the Imperial Treasury would approve of this Government transaction. The UAC were so alarmed at the prospect before the cocoa trade . . . because they could not face the liability of having to buy their . . . share of cocoa at their own risk . . .[18]

The manager went on to say that the question of storage was a disturbing one and that, as he wrote in 1939, the arrangement was expected to last only for one season. It is clear from this description that the government would pay for the cocoa purchase at the end of the season and that the Ministry would ask the firms to sell the cocoa under the direction and at the risk of the government. All of these arrangements were expected to avert local speculation and also to guarantee some income to the farmers and the firms that were operating in an unsure market and shipping environment. As noted previously, only after the government had made these guarantees was UAC ready to go ahead.

As noted before, the firms trading in cocoa considered that the trade would suffer because priorities for shipping would normally not include such luxury goods as cocoa.

During the course of the war, particularly after the United States became actively involved, British ships carrying munitions and equipment sailed from America to England, traveled to West Africa, and came back to the United States with cocoa.[19] Some American ships also carried cocoa, but only those which had already been in the cocoa trade with West Africa before the war.

Some cocoa was burned when shipping space was unavailable, particularly in 1941 and at the close of the war in 1945, when the scraps were destroyed. In all, perhaps only 100,000 tons and certainly not more then 500,000 tons were burned. Cocoa to be burned was determined mainly on the basis of the location at which it was delivered. At the end of the war, as a result of these arrangements, there was no surplus. In answer to questions by Mr. Creech-Jones about the fixed price during the 1939-40 session of £16 16s. per ton at Accra, the Colonial Secretary, Malcolm MacDonald, replied:

It was impossible, in view of the peculiar conditions in West Africa, to determine even the approximate cost of production of cocoa, and it was generally accepted that the price of £16 16s per ton at Gold Coast ports was a very fair price for growers, particularly when it was guaranteed for the whole main crop season. He (the Minister) considered that H.M. Government had acted most generously in this matter, and that the arrangements had conferred considerable benefits on the West African cocoa farmers. He had had no reports of any general dissatisfaction at the price at which cocoa was being bought.

Four years later the Colonial Secretary, Oliver Stanley, announced the increases in price for cocoa:

As a result of a full examination of the position of the cocoa industry in West Africa and in consultation with the governments concerned and the Resident Minister in West Africa, substantial price increases have been announced in the Gold Coast and Nigeria for the next crops.[20]

Certainly from these reports it was assumed that the farmers were receiving a steady price and an increased price from season to season for their product, as reserves were being built up to be distributed after the war through some internal arrangements on the Coast.

On the Coast the Department of Agriculture was in charge of the marketing and shipping controls, including the allotment of shipping space previously approved by the (London) Ministry of Transport and the Produce Board, and made arrangements for the buying of cocoa. In fact, the firms acted as agents for the Department in buying cocoa from the farmers, and the banks handled the arrangements for payments on the direction of either the London Board through Mr. Tansley for the so-called A shippers, or on the Coast through the Department for the B shippers. Normally the banks performed services depending on the particular arrangements prescribed by the government: they provided resources for buying on the Coast, usually in the form of overdrafts; and they channeled payment for A and B shippers, and/or underwrote B shippers' statements when receipts were presented from the warehouses.

The precise procedures were usually as follows: A shippers would declare the amount of cocoa for sale to A. C. Miles, who represented the Department of Agriculture on the Coast. He, in turn, would inform the Ministry in London, where Mr. Tansley would arrange for shipping and sales and would authorize payment. Payments to A shippers were made either by the banks in London or in Accra as prescribed. The West African Cocoa Control Board (later Produce Control Board) in, first, the Ministry of Food, then, later, the Colonial Office would fix the price of cocoa, the allowances for expenses, and the quotas for each firm. The Board would have the advice of the AWAM in London and of the Department of Agriculture, which had consulted with the local AWAM advisory committee.

For B shippers the procedures were similar except that they would have to bring their cocoa to the warehouse and receive a receipt; after the banks had underwritten the purchase, A. C. Miles would proceed with arrangements for shipping and sale through London.

The differences between the price schedule for the A shippers and the schedule for the B shippers were due mainly to the types of services performed. The A shippers' price included all their costs, while the B shippers' price was for the cocoa as delivered to the warehouse. The Government would have to pay for further transport, as well as storage. Most B shippers were in such cocoa areas as Nsawam. They were often risk firms, hence the requirement for delivery to the warehouse.

Although Mr. Tansley was asked to sell cocoa on the terminal market, he preferred selling it on the world market, so that he would not have to buy it back. The most important concerns of the West African Produce Control Board were the regulations concerning cocoa and its control on the Coast. The administrative detail was kept to a minimum by the supervising officials. Decisions were made by personnnel in the Department of Agriculture as shipping became available for cocoa; and before confirmation could be given by England (the Ministry of Food and the Colonial Office), some action had to be taken.[21] For example, it became necessary for the government to underwrite the cost of transport from Accra to Takaradi if a ship were available there and not in Accra. Similarly, when cocoa was destroyed, prices had to be determined.

The Gold Coast officials did have an advisory committee on prices and policies, on which were representatives of AWAM firms. Government participants often felt that the members represented their firm's policies on questions that were brought to the Committee. In addition, it seemed on the Coast that UAC, through Mr. Samuel in London, exerted a great deal of influence on the final pronounce-ments from the Colonial Office. When the government officials communicated to London through UAC cabling services, replies came back within four days, whereas through other channels a reply would take a great deal longer. This situation may have been due to the fact that a personal appeal was made by Samuel to the Colonial Office, which placed the item before the officials immediately; if the government, on the other hand, communicated directly to the Colonial Office or to the Ministry of Food, the communication, even though pressing, would be put aside for other matters.

Under the direction of W. H. Beckett, the division of the Department of Agriculture on the Coast that dealt with cocoa had, since the late twenties, compiled extensive data on cocoa and the firms handling cocoa. Information was drawn from the work of F. G. Emery of the Cooperative Wholesale Society, who had personally collected much of the material. Since the early thirties the department had made forecasts, based on cocoa conditions and prices as published in the Department's reports. From this information it was simple for the officials, as soon as controls were announced for the 1939-40 season, to draw up a list of quotas.[22] Their suggestions were submitted to the AWAM Advisory Committee, which usually approved the recommendations of the division. The division attempted to limit delaying requirements and to press through the shipment of cocoa whenever possible. It was described as a simple authoritarian procedure which was not interrupted or delayed by the committee on the Coast.

London had the final word on all aspects of the controls, and at times local decisions were reversed; this happened, for example, when a single price schedule for both A and B shippers for cocoa that was to be burned was quickly amended to a separate price schedule for each group. Although one of the administrators on the Coast did not see the necessity of two schedules, London continued to overturn any decision that abolished the distinction between A and B shippers.[23]

There was sentiment in favor of the B shippers, yet the Department did not encourage the new firms to deal in cocoa, and for that matter seldom gave quotas to firms not exporting extensively at the beginning of the war. A. G. Leventis was one of the latter.[24] This firm had grown quickly. Although it was suspect because of alleged illegal activity, the Department still granted it a quota according to its shipments, and attempted to allow it shipping space. The A shippers did not often assist it and indeed made difficulties for it. Cocoa, for example, had to be shipped in bags; UAC had a supply of these bags on the Coast, but Leventis, which had earlier left G. B. Ollivant (which had connections with Unilever) did not buy bags from UAC but purchased them from Asia, one report said from Malaya. Since one shipment was consigned to New York, the cost to Leventis was much greater than the cost of UAC bags would have been.[25]

Effect of Business Relations with Governmental Bodies during the War

The war period produced a close partnership between business firms handling cocoa and governmental departments, both in London and in Accra. This was the longest period of such daily contact. Through the suggestions of Cadbury, the Colonial Office implemented the scheme for controls and licensing for the buying of certain products, including cocoa. Personnel for the wartime operations came from the manufacturing and shipping concerns. In fact the Joint West African Committees in England and on the Coast acted as a liaison for the operations of these controls. In dealing with other specific problems, such as war risk insurance and position of intermediaries, the concerns did not succeed as well. It was thought, however, that through the quota system, administered on the Coast in cooperation with AWAM, and the efforts to maintain not more than 2 percent profits after transport, the firms had adequate wartime insurance.[26]

The annual reports and minutes of the Joint West African Committee mention two contacts with governmental departments during 1942. The committee suggested that the Colonial Office support the idea of war risk insurance, but the committee was not satisfied with the response and asked for a meeting concerning the issue. At the end of the year it was noted that some cocoa had been removed from ships, and it was thought that the Ministry of Transport had exerted pressure on the shipping concerns to remove the cocoa. The Ministry of Transport was responsible for allotting shipping space and therefore removed space from cocoa shipments when other supplies seemed more essential for transport.[27]

Controls at the End of the War. The controls on shipping and buying of produce and merchandise were continued until the end of the war much as they were originally conceived in 1939.[28] When the war was over, however, British businesses, particularly concerns in such federations as the Federation of British Business and the Commonwealth Industries Association, were eager for price controls and other regulations to be removed, and now the close working relationship between business and government began to dissolve.

The Firms' Role in Gold Coast Development, 1939-1945. A radical change in the economic activities in the Gold Coast—a change not anticipated by any reports during the thirties—took place in 1939.[30] The change was from little, if any, governmental control to almost complete governmental control of the market. P. T. Bauer describes the marketing procedures as governmental monopolies that were not necessary and suggests that price control alone would have been sufficient to stabilize prices, improve market conditions for the cocoa-buying firms, and bring the producers good prices. Bauer also goes on to say that on the Coast there was suspicion that the governmental monopolies were in reality the firms' pool in disguise.[31]

Bauer, in his work on West African trade, has criticized the controls and marketing arrangements during the war on the ground that there was too much governmental control and too little benefit to the producers. He found that cocoa was maintained at a price relatively low in relation to the world price, though others explained that the farmers continued to plant and harvest cocoa because they began to expect a certain price for cocoa.[32] He failed, however, to ascribe any value to a maintained price, nor to reserved funds to help maintain the prices and to be used for the general social benefit of the farmers and the people of the country.

Bauer criticized marketing arrangements, which tend to monopolize the market and control prices, mainly as deterrents to the farmers receiving the best price for their products. Yet he recognized that fluctuations in market prices have left farmers frequently with wide variations in annual incomes. In order to have as little control over the market as possible, he recommended a sustaining or minimum price under which the produce would not be sold. Such a price would be an average price over a three-year period.

It seems difficult, whether there are controls or not, to see how the farmer would receive an income comparable to the cost of production. The degree of regulations suggested by Bauer in the fifties only slightly fell short of those already afforded by marketing arrangements and plans for stabilization funds in such institutions as dairy marketing in New Zealand. The latter can still result in an efficiently organized producer arrangement, which makes it possible for farmers to receive a sustained income and avoids the ever-present problems of distributors' management of prices. Unfortunately, marketing arrangements on the Gold Coast did not remain independent of governmental intervention, although the farmer did receive a more stable income during the war years and after, through various governmental arrangements.[33]

During the war the price to farmers in the Gold Coast was steady (see above, page 134), and reserves were built up and were to be turned over after the war to the Gold Coast people through new marketing arrangements. Because of the emphasis on winning the war, there was little questioning of wartime controls in Britain or the Gold Coast. The marketing-board arrangements when first established did bring some of the same benefits to the farmers as had wartime controls. The farmers continued to receive at least a minimum price, and reserved funds were used to guarantee the price and to assist with research in cocoa growth, as well as to regularize market procedures. As noted earlier, the firms' profits were controlled by the government's price-setting. The firms were not to make more than 2 percent profit above the price of cocoa to the farmer plus transportation costs.[34]

What was the relative contribution of British business to development in the Gold Coast during the war? With little question the firms supported wartime controls and marketing arrangements. These arrangements led to new and perhaps irreversible conditions in the Gold Coast economy—brought on by government controls. Such controls have since been judged necessary for a country that wishes to develop its economy and achieve political independence quickly. The economic conditions that the firms encouraged during the war were therefore to bring eventually more local control over economic development.

The British firms during the war turned numerous tasks and positions over to Ghanaians. These positions during the thirties had been held by expatriates. The war, without question, gave a boost to the involvement of Ghanaians in the economic and political processes of that country. The firms were not directly consulted on economic, social, and political needs of the people, but Sir Alan Burns, the governor during the war, did receive their suggestions favorably.[35] As for wartime views about the role of the firms, few, if any, critical comments appeared. It was only after the war that local Gold Coast opinion critical of the firms began to circulate. Nor was much written during the War about the motivation of British business. Only after the war did a rash of criticism appear about European business, and it centered on AWAM participation in marketing arrangements during the war.[36] It was this group of British A cocoa shippers which was responsible for establishing the quotas for cocoa sales.

The firms, then, could be termed by some as exploiters because of the way they handled suggestions about quotas—namely by discouraging local firms from developing a cocoa market. The British firms, on the other hand, were in fact not increasing their profits significantly, for cocoa was only shipped when space was available. Government controls acted as a buffer to encourage firms to maintain activity in the cocoa trade until the end of the war, when new marketing arrangements could be developed. In the development of these arrangements, then, arose the innovative contributions of the firms during the Second World War.

4

PLANS FOR POSTWAR COCOA MARKETING

Another major concern of government and business was the planning for postwar marketing. As we have seen, recommendations had been made earlier in the 1938 Royal Commission Report, and two Gold Coast committees had been appointed to consider means of implementing the Commission's proposals. But before any action was possible, World War Two began and wartime controls on marketing and shipping were instituted. During the war a white paper reaffirmed support for a cocoa-marketing board in the Gold Coast for the future. In 1946 such a board was supported again by another white paper and was finally established in 1947.

Recommendations of the 1938 Royal Commission and the Two Government Committees in 1939

In brief the major recommendations of the 1938 Commission focused on the establishment of local cooperative cocoa-buying groups. The operational details were left to the government, farmers, and firms. The Holts records of November 1938 indicate that the buying groups, it was thought, would be organized into at least six regions, each under a regional manager responsible to a general manager. The firms would then buy from all main buying stations where European organizations existed, or from stations indicated by the regional manager. The Cocoa Marketing Board or Farmers Associations would contract with the merchants, and would arrange for advance payments to the farmers, and thus the middleman was expected to disappear. Reactions to the Commission's recommendations were varied.

In the Holts report mention was made of press criticisms and of the firm's reactions:

The main criticisms of the informed British Press seem to me to concentrate on the point that the scheme is probably a generation in advance of its time. If we co-operate with goodwill and the scheme is tried out, it will either prove itself to be a good thing, or it will fail. Nobody can tell which will happen until it is tried. If it succeeds, by which I mean that if it raised the purchasing power of the Gold Coast, then its justification is self-evident. We shall have to adjust ourselves to the evolution of commercial practice and we shall have some reward in the merchandise trade. If it does not succeed in spite of our goodwill, then we shall hear nothing about marketing boards in West Africa for a good many years, and we can get on with our work.[1]

In addition, the firms, in various internal communications, each separately expressed the position that they should not oppose the report, and also noted that the farmers were likely to offer opposition. A Holts report of November 1938 discouraged trade opposition on the following basis:

From the point of view of trade as a whole, if we prevent the report from being implemented, it will always be widely believed that vested interests have wrecked the scheme and are standing in the way of its being given a trial. We shall have public opinion and Government against us. We shall have friction with our customers, and we may, in the last resort, be forced into compliance by legislation.[2]

In regard to Holts' particular situation, the report noted that the firm could continue with less expense if the bush stores (stores in the village and rural areas) were legislated out of existence, and if the agreement were continued in some form but operated solely in respect of English-based firms:

The Paramount Chiefs are all in favour of the grouping and direct marketing of cocoa under their own management. As you are aware, they are not permitted to interfere or take any part in the management of Cooperative Societies. They will do everything in their power to promote the movement as outlined by the Commission providing that they have their fingers, very largely, in the pie.

Unless I am very much mistaken, that is the prelude to further enquiries in regard to the Merchandise Selling Agreement. For the salvation of that Agreement also, I cannot too strongly urge that its operation be transferred wholly to England, that co-operation on the Coast be abolished and that each Member manage his own household.[3]

A February 1939 communication from Accra also indicated that the Paramount Chiefs were in favor of grouping and direct marketing of cocoa under their own management, that the middlemen naturally opposed such suggestions, and that the farmers were suspicious of the Chiefs.[4]

The Governor, on December 10, 1938, authorized the appointment of two committees to consider the collective marketing scheme proposed by the Commission. He appointed the Accra committee himself, and authorized the Chief Commissioner in Kumasi to appoint a similar committee variously known as the Kumasi or Ashanti committee. The committees were to report on the practicality and probable cost of such a scheme, investigate the licensing of buyers and buying stations, and advise whether the farmers could, on the basis of the London prices, arrive at a rough estimate of the correct local price. The committees, which finally reported in April 1939, were composed so as to have representation from each of the groups concerned with cocoa. The Accra committee consisted of the Hon. A. C. Duncane Johnstone, Provincial Commissioner, as chairman; Mr. F. G. Emery of the Co-operative Wholesale Society; Mr. A. C. Miles from the Department of Agriculture; the Hon. Nana Sir Ofori Atia, K.B.E., a Paramount Chief; and Mr. W. W. Barnhill, Assistant Colonial Secretary, as secretary. Later appointees included the Hon. Nana Tsibu Darku IX, and Mr. R. Barrow for the Accra Chamber of Commerce. The Kumasi (Ashanti) committee included Captain J. C. Warrington, Chief Commissioner, as chairman; S. Stead from Agriculture; and Jack More of the United Africa Company, as secretary. Later, A. F. Bray of United Africa Company's produce department was asked to join, and Mr. Hindeman of the Swiss Africa Trading Company was co-opted.[5] The UAC appointments to the Kumasi committee were later criticized because of UAC's opposition to the selling of cocoa on a uniform scale by African farmers. The secretary, Mr. More of UAC, noted, however, that he was asked to serve as secretary only after the resignation of the first appointee, and that Mr. Bray was brought in to represent the firms only when there had been several other refusals.[6]

The firms that had been parties to the 1937 Agreement were not directly represented on the Accra committee. Cadburys had been asked to send a representative, but the firm declined because their major concern was with the manufacture and not the purchase of cocoa. John Cadbury and William Hood of Cadburys did make a presentation to the committee, however, requesting that the government assure the shippers that no cocoa marketing scheme would be introduced without considering the trade. The secretary of the Accra committee sent a letter to the Secretary of State for the Colonies requesting that the Co-operative Society and the firms interested in West African cocoa trade be heard before the recommendations of the committees were implemented. In the Secretary of State's reply was a commitment to give the interested firms full opportunity to express their views after the committee reports were received.[7]

When both committees reported in April 1939, they concluded that the scheme was workable and gave an estimate of the expenses involved. The Ashanti (Kumasi) committee concluded that difficulties such as the financing of the scheme would present major problems.[8] A minority report, submitted by F. G. Emery from the Co-operative Societies (CWS), did emerge from the Accra committee. It indicated that the committee had failed to consider the opposition by the farmers to a marketing scheme or to any compulsory scheme for marketing:

The two African members of the Ashanti Committee made no bones about stressing to the Committee the fact that (*a*) producers in Ashanti were unanimous in their objection to Chiefs having any function in relation to the marketing of their cocoa, and (*b*) that the producers would resist any Government legislation just as much as they would Chiefs' legislation in connection with compulsory methods of marketing their cocoa. How truly they represent the native element in their views, it is difficult for me to say, but there can be no doubt that generally speaking the farmer and broker are dead against any scheme of compulsory central marketing. It remains to be seen whether Ofori Atta and the other chiefs can overcome their objections by propaganda or, as they did in the case of the hold-up, by fear.[9]

Mr. Emery also quoted the Director of Agriculture, Mr. Auchinlech, who suggested that the Agricultural Co-operative Societies should be the basis of the association for marketing and that the Department of Agriculture should have ultimate direction of the scheme. Mr. Emery, of course, supported this arrangement in his report.

Some members of the Ashanti committee were also reported to have noted the farmers' opposition to such schemes. In a brief description of the Committee's work a general statement about the problems is given:

In Ashanti the committee has had some seven meetings. They are following the line of studying each individual item in the recommendations of the Commission and endeavouring to draft a practical scheme that is calculated to meet each item. There are innumerable difficulties and so far little has emerged towards an actual draft scheme.[10]

In an April communication from UAC a more detailed note about local opposition to a marketing board scheme was advanced:

At both places they have been able to secure meetings of members of the Committee with farmers, which have brought out unmistakably the fact that generally speaking the Africans do not understand the scheme and would certainly not welcome any scheme which (*a*) was compulsory; (*b*) left it uncertain what price they would secure and when they would be paid; (*c*) did not render it possible for them to secure advances. It should now be impossible for the local Government to plead that the proposals have the support of the African farmer which the Commission considered was essential.

In Kumasi already the committee has adopted schedules showing that marketing under the Commission's scheme will cost from £2.4.0 to £2.12.0 per ton, apart from the Merchants; deductions for overheads if the cocoa was disposed of through them and that for the Kumasi crop of 90,000 tons the Government would have to find some £320,000 by way of capital, without taking into account the additional capital which would be necessary if substantial advances were to be made to the producer or the liabilities if a speculative sales policy were pursued.[11]

Various articles and editorials in the newspapers on the Coast indicated why the farmers were suspicious of the marketing board scheme. In an editorial dated April 11th, 1939, the *Spectator Daily* urged that the cocoa industry be as "unfettered as possible without licensing, however, should the farmer agree to a group system then the groups should supply their own bye-laws with the privilege of selling to whomever they wished". On the same date the *African Morning Post* expressed the view that the Buying Agreement was still operating, "although indirectly and imperceptibly". Despite this accusation the agreement, as noted in the last chapter,[12] did not go back into operation after the spring of 1938: "There was no agreement or understanding written or verbal between parties to Cocoa Agreement after abandonment of Cocoa Agreement, November 1939, up to July, 1946; neither has there been any since".[13]

On April 15 the *Spectator Daily* urged that the experience of the English and Irish marketing boards be viewed before such systems were supported on the Coast. The African farmers were not opposed to a collective marketing system in principle, according to the May 19 *Morning Post,* but were only opposed to any system that might deprive them eventually of individual rights and privileges "resulting in restricting their freedom to dispose of their property wherever or whenever they chose to do so. ... African farmers [sic] welcome that system of collective marketing which enables him to dictate his own price in the same way the merchant does, without restricting his freedom of action." On the 25th of that month it was noted in the *Spectator Daily* that the Governor had informed the Secretary of State that no modification in the marketing scheme was possible for the 1939-40 crop, since the committee reports had only just been received.

The Committees reported just a few months before Britain entered the Second World War. Official discussions thus turned to wartime controls and did not return to arrangements for cocoa marketing on a more permanent basis until 1944.

White Paper of 1944

In a review of cocoa control from 1939 to 1943, the Secretary of State for the Colonies proposed that the selling of cocoa in West Africa should not revert to the chaotic prewar situation in which price speculation could so easily exist.[14] He went on to recommend the establishment of organizations "empowered by law to purchase the total production of cocoa, prescribe the prices to be paid to the producers, and to be responsible for the disposal of the cocoa. These organizations would be established by, and responsible to, the Colonial Governments, and would be required to act as trustees for the producers." He discussed the Cooperative Movement and the relation of these organizations:

The development of this movement [the Co-operative] remains a cardinal object of government policy, and indeed it is felt that the growth of the movement may be greatly strengthened and accelerated through the operation of the scheme that is now proposed. Secondly, the constitution and composition of the proposed local organization are not to be regarded as final or permanent. Quite apart from such variations in the proposals set out above as may on further consideration seem appropriate before the scheme is brought into being in 1945, the organizations may be expected to change and to develop with experience, both in the direction of increased and more direct representation of the producers themselves, and in the light of the development of general international commodity policy.[15]

The Secretary of State saw the West Africa cocoa industry fitting into an international cooperative movement:

Thirdly, the scheme, while designed to meet the special circumstances of the West African cocoa industry, can be fitted in without difficulty as a part of any wider international scheme that may later be established. Should it be deemed desirable to institute some international organization for dealing with the problems of the production or marketing of cocoa, His Majesty's Government would be willing to participate in such an organization, and it is considered that its operation would not be incompatible with the existence of producers' marketing agencies such as those now proposed for British West Africa. Finally, the proposals involved no change whatever in the arrangements whereby the entire British West African output of cocoa is now available for allocation by the Combined Food Board in Washington,[16] and the decisions of that body will continue to be put into effect as hitherto.[17]

Although the proposal was to be submitted for legislative action and then go into operation during the 1945-46 season, the appropriate steps were not taken for that season, nor for the next. In November 1946 another statement reiterated the marketing board proposals, explaining that the experience of the war years demonstrated that the government could "achieve a stabilization of seasonal prices for the West African cocoa producer, despite heavy fluctuations in supply and demand, yet any permanent organization should report from West Africa, not from London".[18] The colonial government, not His Majesty's Government, should be responsible for the operation of the marketing scheme.

According to the report, the board on the Coast was to have ten members, representing producers from the Colony and Ashanti, the chambers of commerce, and the cocoa manufacturers. The functions of the board:

(*a*)   to fix the seasonal prices payable to producers.
(*b*)   to determine purchase arrangements and issue licenses to buyers; and
(*c*)   to set up and maintain the necessary executive machinery for purchasing, shipping and selling all cocoa purchased.[19]

Seasonal buying licenses were to be issued to agents. These recommendations for the board were essentially realized in the board established in 1947.

Reactions of the Firms

There is ample evidence that the government in London had, in 1944, consulted with affected parties about the marketing board scheme: these parties included those firms and manufacturers that had been concerned with the marketing of cocoa and in fact had acted as buying agents for the government under wartime controls.[20]

The Colonial Office, early in September, sent a statement regarding the proposed White Paper on the future of West African cocoa marketing to the cocoa manufacturers. Three meetings between the London Cocoa Committee of the Association of West African Merchants and various colonial officials, including the Secretary of State for the Colonies, were held between September 22 and the end of November 1944. The West African cocoa merchants and manufacturers had ample opportunity through correspondence and meetings, to express their views about proposals for future governmental controls and organizations for the trade.

Frank Samuel was the spokesman for the AWAM committee. His September statements and December letter focused on three concerns:

(*a*) the disregard for consumer interests;
(*b*) the failure to define the powers of the Marketing Boards; and
(*c*) the omission from discussion of the role for the established firms.[21]

In answer to these points, the secretary emphasized that the report on the West African Cocoa Marketing, issued in November 1944, primarily reviewed the existing wartime marketing scheme and recommended general procedures for the Colonies to follow in establishing marketing boards once wartime controls ceased.[22] He announced that around £2,700 thousand would be turned over to the established boards and anticipated that these funds would be used to reduce fluctuations in prices rather than to assume control of the entire marketing program in West Africa. The Secretary of State, however, firmly stated that the Royal Commission report could not lay down the details for an organizational scheme within each colony but could only recommend a general procedure. The governments in each colony would present the details.

Firms not directly involved with the cocoa trade, however, were not consulted by the government. This was evident in the discussions of the Joint West African Committee (Liverpool). The latter firms expressed interest mainly because of the possibility of government entrance into the trading area and eventual take-over.

After the release of the 1944 White Paper, representatives of the West African firms expressed a diversity of views, ranging from complete opposition toward any government control to the accusation, by the firms involved in cocoa trading, that the paper supported a producers' cartel and not government trading. The West African sections of the Liverpool, Manchester, and London Chambers of Commerce adopted similar resolutions supporting parts of the White Paper. The Liverpool section issued the first statement approving the objectives of the White Paper dealing with the stabilization of the buying price of cocoa and cocoa research but opposing the establishment of a state trading monopoly and some of the methods of achieving these objectives.[23] In the same month, February 1945, the Executive Council of the Association of British Chambers of Commerce sent a resolution with similar sentiments to appropriate governmental departments. This resolution stated:

The Executive Council of the Association of British Chambers of Commerce having considered the Government White Paper—Cmd. 6554, Report of Cocoa Control in West Africa, 1939-1943 and Statement on Future Policy— welcome the general objective of the Paper which appears to be:

(1) to protect the West African cocoa producer against fluctuations of price and to secure for him a reasonable return on the cost of production; and (2) to make adequate provision for cocoa research in the West African Colonies but condemns as dangerous, unworkable and unnecessary the scheme proposed to attain these ends, which constitutes the establishment of a Government-sponsored producers' monopoly with full statutory powers.

　　Their reasons were:
(*a*)　The necessary commercial organisations already exist to buy, transport, and market cocoa efficiently.
(*b*)　The present British Government holds no mandate from the country to nationalise commercial enterprise.
(*c*)　There is no protection for the interests of cocoa consumers.
(*d*)　There is no limitation to the powers to be entrusted to the Board.[24]

　　The London and Manchester sections adopted similar resolutions during April .[25]
　　With the issuance of the September 1944 report, the Colonial Office began to consult with firms involved in the cocoa trade. Its statement about the proposed future policy for the marketing of West African cocoa suggested the establishment of machinery to purchase the total production of cocoa, to prescribe the prices to be paid to producers, and to be responsible for sales.[26] Such proposals "constitute an adaption of war-time machinery to bring it one stage nearer to objective of co-operative selling . . ."
　　The 1944 report gives the Colonial Office's approval for cocoa marketing arrangements in West Africa. The 1939 recommendations of the Coast Committees and the Colonial Office's 1944 statement lay the basis for the Gold Coast statute of 1947 establishing a cocoa marketing board.

The Firms and Policy

By 1939 the British firms, fresh from the cocoa hold-up negotiations and their failure to float a quota control agreement, gave evidence of growing "enlightened" views toward the cocoa farmer and toward controls of the Gold Coast market through governmental arrangement. The form of this control was moving toward a marketing board arrangement for buying and selling, and toward cooperative efforts among farmers. The firms pragmatically realized that they could not go back to their agreements to control the cut-throat features of the market, and thus they explicitly supported a trial of the marketing board recommendations of the Royal Commission. Their "enlightened" attitude, then, included the realization that to maintain a trading situation on the Coast they had to go along with proposals for controls that would be acceptable to government and the farmer. In addition, the people of the Coast, in order to buy European goods, needed some form of prosperity. The farmers were the ones who still viewed any control of the market, either by the firms or by the government, as questionable, on the grounds that they, the farmers, would lose their freedom to decide to whom to sell.

The firms' representatives in London and Liverpool, however, by 1944 were questioning the type of governmental controls being considered and particularly opposed a state trading monopoly. The representatives continued to support in principle some form of control over the market. They also raised questions about how much, if at all, the government had considered the consumers' interests.

The local trading firms in 1946-47 were still attempting to establish themselves, yet governmental controls during the war tended to favor the British firms as A shippers, even though local firms could theoretically emerge in the trade.[27]

Throughout the wartime negotiations on the future organization for the cocoa trade, the Secretary of State for the Colonies continued to support local cooperation on the Coast, as well as marketing boards, which, according to the Royal Commission report of 1944, would be using machinery and controls similar to those already established for wartime trade. He explicitly told the firms that the details of operations should be left to each colony to work out locally. The 1947 Gold Coast Act did bring in a marketing board to purchase and sell cocoa, and continued to make room for the British firms as buying agents.

The firms thus, in an atmosphere of necessity, reflected an enlightened voice toward the farmers' interests. Again we have the intimate interlocking of the profit-seeking motive with an innovative characteristic of business concern for the farmers' welfare. These two motives are so intertwined here that the contribution of each to the actions of the firms cannot be quantified. The firms realized that to have trade they had to accept and try governmental controls and a marketing arrangement not of their own making. Wartime controls led easily into these arrangements and gave the firms the opportunity to define their own positions.

The farmer remained concerned about controls over his option to sell to anyone he wished. This time the control would be by the government, not by the firms. Could the farmer really understand the international market and how dependent he was on any organization—be it private, cooperative, or governmental—for his sales? Could any system be created to afford him the type of trading system he desired?[28]

5

POSTWAR DISSENSION AND CHANGE,
1947-1948

For the first few years after the war, West Africa was concerned about the marketing of cocoa, and, like Britain and other nations at the close of the war, about spiraling prices and short supplies. These years marked the onset of local unrest in the Gold Coast. This unrest, which sprang first of all from economic dissatifactions, was diverted by the new African leaders into political demands.

Local wrath was soon directed toward expatriate firms in West Africa, in particular those which, like UAC and Holts, were involved in selling scarce goods. The cocoa purchasers were criticized for the quota system that during the war determined which firms would buy and ship cocoa. The shippers had been selected mainly from among the low-risk firms that could handle economic uncertainties of the wartime trade.[1] It was felt that this system had discriminated against the smaller African firms.

During this same postwar period, the Colonial Office in London was developing new policies toward the colonies. These policy changes were partly the result of studies that were made during the war of Gold Coast developments in education, medical care, and self-government. Economic studies were also started by 1940 on the Volta River project. The new Labour government in London now emphasized labor organization, cooperatives, and further steps toward self-government. These major changes in Colonial policies under the Labour Party are documented both in Colonial Office papers and in the testimonies of former colonial officials in the Gold Coast. Yet, as noted below (pages 100-101) even with this emphasis it was not expected that self-government would come for several decades.[2]

The governorship of the colony was in a state of transition during the postwar period. Governor Alan Burns, who had served during some of the war period and who was responsible for the promulgation of a constitution providing for increased African membership in the Legislative Council, left the Coast early in 1947 and was only replaced in late 1947 by Governor Gerald Creasy, a career employee of the Colonial Office without field experience before the appointment.[3] Governors up to this time had usually had such experience.

Many on the Coast, including the firms' representatives, were surprised in early 1948 at the magnitude and length of the rioting and disturbances that occured when returned servicemen were turned from marching to the Governor's castle, although the route had been agreed upon by the government. The Commission reporting on the disturbances indicated, however, that colonial officials certainly should have been prepared for such disturbances, particularly if they had taken into consideration the abilities of the farmers to organize in the 1930's, as well as the general climate of opinion in 1947 about the prices and lack of supplies. Certainly the prices in England were rising and were being reflected in the price rises on the Coast.[4] At no time before had there been such large public protests in the Gold Coast. Even the crises of 1938 did not produce the types of unrest evident in 1948.

The changes in marketing arrangements and the unrest over prices were thus among the most important postwar events in the Coast. We turn first to the establishment of the marketing board and then to the settlements on prices and supplies.

The Cocoa Marketing Board

By the time of the 1946 report by the Secretary of State for the Colonies on the marketing of cocoa in West Africa, most affected parties, including the British firms and the Gold Coast cocoa farmers, had aired their views about marketing arrangements in discussions with the Colonial Office and the Gold Coast Government. It was believed that the suggested marketing board would take care of many of the trade abuses existing before the Second World War, including the crucial problems of fluctuating prices, brokers' abuses, and fair returns to the farmers.

By 1946 the firms dealing with cocoa buying had accepted the government's marketing board concept. This acceptance came about mainly as a result of the firm's experiences during the war as agents of the government and as a result of not seeing another solution to the market difficulties that would be acceptable to all the affected parties. The firms thus did not hinder the localization of economic controls in the Coast government, but by 1947 were encouraging that step.

The Board was established by a Gold Coast Act in 1947 and was to have four main functions:

(*a*) to control and fix, with the prior approval of the Governor in Council, the prices to be paid from time to time to Gold Coast producers for their cocoa;

(*b*) to purchase cocoa and to do all things necessary for and in connection therewith;

(*c*) to appoint licensed buying agents for the purchase of cocoa on behalf of the board;

(*d*) to sell cocoa and to do all things necessary for and in connection with the selling, exporting, shipping, and storage of cocoa.[5]

The established European firms became licensed buyers of the Board and worked in competition with other licensed buyers, including the Cocoa Purchasing Company, which was formed as a subsidiary of the Board in 1952. After the Board's establishment, the firms made presentations on any specific problems, when necessary, to the administrator on the Coast and to the London office of the Board, which sold cocoa on the world market. They no longer went to the Colonial Office or to the government in London on problems of West African trade.

As a result of the marketing scheme, the producers were able to realize a stable price for cocoa each season despite fluctuations in world prices. The Gold Coast producer realized £51.6.8 per ton in 1947, £74.13.4 in 1948, £121.6.8 in 1949, a decline to £84 in 1950, and a rise to £140.12.5 by·1957.[6]

The British government turned over the reserve funds collected by the West African Producers Control Board during the war. This fund amounted to £1,377,233 for the 1943-44 and 1944-45 seasons. Parliament also voted to turn over to the new board similar sums for the 1945-46 and 1946-47 seasons. The Board began in 1947 with a reserve fund of approximately £13½ million.[7] Cadburys, in its 1948 report, noted that the Board had, by that time, accumulated £34 million surplus.

The accumulated profits of the Cocoa Control were taken over by the Board, and it is expected to finish this year's working with a surplus of £34 million. A portion of this will be reserved to finance next year's marketing. A further portion, amounting to £16 million will be used to establish a stabilization fund in order to guarantee a minimum price of 25/- per load to the farmer for 5 years.[8]

The producers did not see any direct benefit of these funds. They thought of them as benefiting the welfare of the community as it improved through efforts of the Gold Coast government, and the Ghanaian government, particularly after 1959, which would use the reserve funds not only for stabilization purposes but also for development programs.

Some producer representation was provided on the Marketing Board, but it was not adequate at first to give the farmer a sense of identity with the Board's decisions. One to one communications between the Board and each farmer did not develop, easily. Such a feature is a necessity for a smoothly operating, producer-marketing board. The farmers, according to the press, were resentful when they were not consulted about the allocation of cocoa profits to other activities, such as higher education. From time to time there was discussion about use of the funds to relieve farmers in debt and to help farmers ruined by swollen-shoot disease.[9]

Also the farmers still found it necessary to borrow money before the season's crops were sold. Cadburys reports continued to mention money sent to the coast for loans.[10] The most noteworthy developments during the decade, according to these reports, were the change to capable African personnel on the Board, and the continued need for disease control and replanting to ensure the crop size. The Gold Coast had been responsible for about half the world's supply of cocoa in 1938 and continued to supply a large portion of the crop, approximately one third in the 1950's. Because of disease and reduced planting during the war, this proportion, however, had been reduced.[11]

In April 1952 W. M. Hood of Cadburys and Lloyd Owen of Rowntrees visited the Coast and on behalf of the manufacturers expressed their concern for controlling the swollen-shoot disease that had developed after cutting out diseased trees had been suspended in 1951. The only control for swollen-shoot disease, since its inception in the thirties, was cutting the diseased trees. Individual farmers resisted cutting their own trees. The Colonial administration conducted educational campaigns (as did the later Ghanaian-led governments) yet resistance persisted. Upon the election of Nkrumah's party in 1951, the government appealed to the cocoa farmers through a program called the New Deal, which suspended cutting-out but did not look for another way to control the disease. Soon, however, cutting-out was again being sanctioned by the Gold Coast government. Hood and Owen from the manufacturers, in April 1952, urged the Prime Minister to resume the policy:

In this short visit it has been impossible to travel widely, but our numerous contacts every hour of every day we have been here have convinced us that your efforts to enlighten the farmers and the people of the Gold Coast have resulted in the formation of a new climate of opinion which appears to us to be ready at this moment for strong action and clear leadership.

But since organised cutting-out was suspended there has been a marked spread of disease and much ground has been lost. Cocoa which could have earned you finance has gone forever, and we cannot escape an increasing feeling of grave concern for the future of the cocoa crop.

We cannot find any evidence that the New Deal Campaign will achieve by itself, valuable as it has been, the volume of cutting-out which we believe you desire, and we venture to express our conviction, as somewhat outside but interested and sympathetic observers, that the time is ripe now for clear leadership directed to the comprehensive action which is inescapable.

In particular we refer to the position in Ashanti where it is still possible to establish control over the whole most valuable areas by a few weeks cutting-out work. We find it difficult to give our friends at home any understandable reason why so simple a process is not immediately applied to save so much.[12]

Paul S. Cadbury continued to express concern about the quality of cocoa after his visit in 1956:

When I was in the Gold Coast in 1947 I was pessimistic about the survival of the cocoa industry. What should be done to save it was well-recognised but the difficulties seemed to be insuperable. Those difficulties have been largely surmounted, and as the solution of the problems of the future presents fewere social and political hurdles than the containing of swollen shoot, I believe that they will be crossed.

As I said in a short broadcast which I gave over the Gold Coast radio: "The most important men in the Gold Coast are its 350,000 cocoa farmers; the economy of the whole country depends on their work. Gold Coast cocoa has a fine reputation and well fermented Accra [the usual term for cocoa as prepared by the farmer for sale to agents] sets a standard for the rest of the world. Nevertheless, none of us must rest on our past reputation. I sell the chocolate of which cocoa is a vital ingredient, and the maintenance of quality is the most important single factor in its manufacture. What manufacturers want is good, well-fermented Grade I, and only that should command the full-price. If the Gold Coast farmer looks after his cocoa, and sprays, ferments and dries it properly and plants more young trees, his own and the country's prosperity is assured".[13]

The cocoa manufacturers, including Cadburys, soon after the war disassociated themselves from the merchant firms and continued with their campaign to improve quality of cocoa by fighting swollen-shoot disease and by emphasizing as noted by Paul Cadbury, the importance of the cocoa farmer. The merchant firms, on the other hand, were preoccupied with the unrest caused by shortages and high prices in the Gold Coast. As the concept of a marketing board became more acceptable, the manufacturers and the merchants no longer made common cause of controlling the fluctuating and unstable cocoa trade. The marketing board seemed the only solution to the marketing problems that would be accepted by all affected parties. During the war the firms had expressed concern about the marketing board concept, but after discussions with the Colonial Secretary in 1944, they went along with the proposal in 1947. Many of the reservations expressed by the firms were like those later emphasized by P. T. Bauer in his critiques of the marketing arrangements.[14]

Martindale and Sachs Commissions

In 1946 a commission headed by M. H. Martindale was appointed by Governor Burns to inquire into allegations made against certain officials in the Supplies and Customs departments and their relation with A. G. Leventis and his company in procuring import licenses. Reporting on December 30, 1946, the commission concluded that the director of supplies. H. W. R. Chandler, had endeavored to restrict imports and to ensure that the colony received its share of essential supplies, but that he had not adequately supervised his subordinates.

On the other hand, the comptroller of customs, W. E. Conway, and his assistant, A. D. W. Allen, had directed a policy of controls markedly favourable to a small group of importers, and Leventis Company had in fact benefited from these polices from 1944 to 1946. The Commission indicated the possibilty that A. G. Leventis had engaged in bribery, particularly in his dealings with Mr. Allen.[15]

These allegations were repudiated by the named officials and by A. G. Leventis. Another Commission of Enquiry was established in 1947 and headed by Eric Sachs. A report still longer than that of 1946 was turned over to the newly arrived Governor on February 14, 1948. This commission found that A. D. W. Allen had been responsible for irregularities when he was in charge of the Import Licensing Branch from July 1944 to May 1946. The report went on to say, however, that: "It is . . . incorrect to suggest that the lapse from integrity involved more than one official, that it was deliberately fostered by the Head of the Department, or that it was such a scale that it upset the whole Government policy".[16] In regard to A. G. Leventis and Company, the commission concluded that the allegations of the Martindale Commission about the company before May 1944 were not supportable, but that a number of substantial allegations concerning activities after May 1944 were true, including the one "in which the Company was proved to be the beneficiary of improper favours bestowed by Mr. Allen i.e., the series of R.W.L.'s the trend of the allocation of Import Licenses, and the transfer to the Company of the tobacco originally consigned to Mr. Acquaye. Generally speaking these favours were known to the Company to be given in breach of Mr. Allen's duties—and the Company resorted to corruption in respect of them."[17]

The position regarding Leventis and Company was summed up as follows:

a Company may well be entitled to try and persuade a Government Official to exercise his legitimate discretion in its favour: but the moment that the exercise of that discretion on the part of that Official must involve a breach of duty, the Company is clearly acting improperly in trying to secure the favour. When the favours and breaches of duty are the subject of corrupt practices as between the Company and the Official—as was the case between A. G. Leventis & Co. Ltd. and Mr Allen—the offence is necessarily and invariably one of gravity.[18]

It was also concluded that Mr. Leventis personally was a party to the company's actions.

In conclusion, the commission indicated that it would make no recomendations for action because it was only appointed to investigate the validity of the allegations against officials in the Supplies and Customs departments and about A. G. Leventis. The commission did, however, indicate the difficulties arising from such privileged positions:

The existence of visible privileges which cannot be manifestly justified not infrequently causes such resentment that it contributes to the commencement of some wrong-doing: the wrong-doing is in no way to be condoned for that reason—but if its origins are understood its degree can be the better assessed and any future occurrence the more easily obviated.

Having stated the above facts, it is proper to emphasize once more that from the files placed before me it is clear that it was no part of the policy of Government either to create or to preserve the advantages mentioned above. Its policy of even-handed treatment was, however, not sufficiently actively implemented by those who dealt with supplies and their allocation.[19]

It commented earlier about special favors to Leventis:

As previously observed, however, the improper receipt of the above favours by the Company occurred after the end of 1943—and by then A. G. Leventis & Co. Ltd. had had to witness a series of events, each in itself resulting in a differentiation between AWAM firms and the Company; and each time the difference was against the Company. However inevitable these decisions may have been and however fair were the intentions of those who took them . . . the reasons for certain of them were at the time far from manifest and they resulted in a genuine feeling by members of A. G. Leventis & Co. Ltd. that it had been unfairly treated.[20]

These reports give some indication of the kinds of allegations, true and false, being made about AWAM, the new companies, and the administration of customs and import controls after the war on the Coast and just before the disturbances of 1948. Leventis and other non-AWAM firms were frequently represented in the press as firms that fought for free trade on behalf of the consumer. Little reference was made in the press to the findings of the Martindale and Sachs Commissions. At the time that each report appeared, copies for distribution became very scarce.[21]

The Disturbances of 1948

The march upon Government House (Christianborg Castle), the fatal shooting of two persons, and the riots and looting of stores all came upon the Gold Coast government and the European firms suddenly and, for some, completely by surprise.[22]

The demonstrations resulted in part from the governor's decision not to receive in person an ex-servicemen's petition. Traditionally the chief or person viewed by the Africans as the source for governmental decision-making in the Gold Coast received personal petitions from the people. The unrest flared as the police turned the marchers away from the Governor's Castle, and when two marchers were shot the demonstrations increased. The rioting also reflected the disappointment of the Accra people with the actual level of prices posted the night before. These prices were nonetheless higher than the people had been led to believe they would be.

The returned servicemen and other Africans were critical of the governor's decision not to receive the ex-servicemen, and some twenty years later in discussions about the disturbances they continued to recall with disfavor this decision. Even some of the firms' agents thought the governor's decision did not reflect adequate knowledge of the local situation. The agents were themselves not prepared for such an outburst: on former occasions extensive dialogues had preceded any form of mass demonstration.[23] Had the Governor received the marchers, the disquiet about short supplies and high prices would probably not have grown into disturbances.

After the rioting started, the Government tried to protect the firms and stop the disturbances. Wherever possible, stores were closed by the firms' management before looting could take place.[24] Although the larger firms could handle their losses, those suffered by the Indian and Syrian merchants were irredeemable.[25]

Causes of the Disturbances

The economic causes cited most frequently for the disturbances were short supplies of goods, high prices, black marketing, unemployment of returned soldiers, and the inadequacies in West Africa of price control and marketing.[26]

A study made in 1947 aptly described each of these problems:

1. Although these notes have been given this title [The Gold Coast riots] it cannot be assumed that the immediate crises is short-run: the grievances that have been expressed by the boycott and riots are symptoms of factors that will arise again as development expenditure increases.
2. These grievances are two: (*a*) the rising prices of goods; (*b*) the unemployment of certain groups, especially at the moment, ex-soldiers. . . . The most serious bottleneck in Africa is that of distribution, and the consequent inelasticity of supplies, especially of food, leads invariably to a sharp rise in prices in any development area. [e.g., the mines in their early years: more recently, the railway construction camps of Kanyeribo]. The first consequence of such expenditure or of any other increase of mass purchasing power, such as a rise in cocoa prices, is an inflation of retail margins. Thus there is little increase of real income for the majority in such cases. While this may be inevitable with imports, the measures outlined may render more even their distribution. Further successful price-control would leave the mass consumer with some savings, or perhaps lead to higher food intake if the increased food supplies became available.[27]

Another report details specific unfavorable views about AWAM in the press on the Coast:

The continuance of the policy of allocating import quotas to the firms of the AWAM on the basis of their import records in the years 1937-1941 has been the main target for Gold Coast press criticism in the period under review. This principle of "Past Performance", it has been argued, has allowed AWAM firms a virtual monopoly of imported goods, excluded non-AWAM firms and small African firms from the trade, and caused artificial scarcity, high prices and profiteering, especially in cloth. The Gold Coast press has followed this line in reporting the proceedings of the Martindale Commission and the Sachs inquiry. Persistence with AWAM after the war has been presented as an attempt to perpetuate the strangle-hold of certain European firms, especially the U.A.C., on the Gold Coast economy, and to bar the way for African commercial advancement. AWAM has been the scapegoat for the rigours of inflation which is attributed to price fixing and cornering supplies by AWAM.[28]

The firms most involved in the events surrounding the disturbances were the importers of goods in rare supply, including textiles, a commodity in constant demand. AWAM was accused of being the instrument for maintaining a scarcity of goods, thus increasing consumer prices on the Coast. In addition, it was popularly thought that the government condoned the actions of the merchants, as it gave little evidence of attempting to alleviate the situation.

The one firm most frequently accused by the press of contributing to the scarcity of commodities and the maldistribution of goods was UAC, probably because it was one of the largest distributors in the Gold Coast, handling approximately 65 percent of the European trade:

During the past three years the independent press of Nigeria and the Gold Coast attacked the UAC unanimously and consistently. The main theme running through a variety of detailed criticisms is that UAC is the leading firm in a monopolistic ring which, by cornering the most of the import and export trade of the Coast, has made fabulous profits for British shareholders and impoverised the miserable African. The ring is presented as consisting of UAC and the Royal Niger Company—both being controlled by Lever Brothers. UAC in turn dominates the Association of West African Merchants. Thus the simple equation presented to the public is AWAM, alias UAC, alias Lever Brothers, equals monopolistic exploitation on behalf of British capital, trade and industry.[29]

One clerk concerned about the commodities crises wrote to UAC:

I am surprise how all your managers are so corrupted in black marketing in all the various stations—serious and dangerous things are going on in Accra and Nsawam and Akuse—The worst is Accra and Nsawam—The managers have special people among the company's customers and more of non-customers before—These are supplied with key commodities particularly cottons and the profits are shared 50-50 . . . You cannot therefore help these people to be so wicked to make money amongst themselves.[30]

As early as 1942 the Accra General Manager urged the retail stores to

bear in mind that Government has wide powers to punish severely those who are convicted of breaking the laws made to control the prices of goods, and any storekeeper who so offends does so not only as an individual, but also as an employeé of the Company. In the event of such a breach of loyalty, the Company could not fail to take the strongest possible action. Any storekeeper who is found selling goods at inflated prices either himself, or through any other person whom he permits to make sales, will in addition to any sentence imposed by the court, be liable to instant dismissal and will be automatically debarred from further employment with this Company, or any of its Associated Companies.[31]

It was also shown that many complaints about inflated prices had been received by the governmeht and the trading firms.

F. J. (later Sir Frederick) Pedler, a UAC representative from London, took a lead in having a public statement on prices printed in the local press.[32] Certain of these prices were agreed to in January before the riots occurred, and all were agreed to in a meeting on February 21 of the Boycott Committee led by Nii Bonne, a businessman and Accra Chief; the Chiefs; the Chamber of Commerce; and the Colonial Secretary. George Cole (later Lord Cole and Chairman of Unilever) explained in detail to the Commission the prices on textiles which were controlled by the government through an agreement with the Chamber of Commerce in 1945. The prices of the best quality textiles were the ones that were the focus of the Boycott Committee's attack, which was declared effective on January 26. UAC had been charging for their best textiles the maximum rate, which was not more than 75 per cent above the duty-paid cost. At the meetings it was agreed to reduce this margin to 50 per cent for the next three months, as a trial period. The press announced that textile prices would be reduced by one third on February 28. UAC did reduce their prices; however the crowds in the stores in some of the larger towns became unruly because among them were some men who shouted that the prices had not been reduced sufficiently. The stores were closed. When they reopened, the goods were offered at the same prices, and business continued to be good into April.[33]

UAC was the only firm to present testimony to the Commission of Enquiry (under the Chairmanship of Aiken Watson; its report was later referred to as the Watson Report). Cole presented the statements when he and F. J. Pedler were on the Coast in April. They went out to observe for the firms and to appear, if necessary, before the Commission of Enquiry.

In a brief summary of underlying causes of the disturbances, George Cole, in his testimony prepared for the Commission, mentioned three major problem areas—political, economic, and social. He defined these areas as follows:

The causes, direct and indirect, of the disorders are obviously complex. We set out below what in our opinion were the main underlying causes, but we shall endeavour to show that many of the grievances arose from misconceptions, accidental or political, economic and social.[34]

Under political causes Cole mentioned the stimulation by the press of considerable political feeling. He also attributed the rise in national feeling to the numbers of African students abroad and the concessions given to Africans in the Legislative Council. His description follows:

The Commission will need no comment on the phenomenon of the flowing tide of nationalism sweeping the world, and in particular its effect on the less developed nations of the British Empire. In this connection, the increasing numbers of African students going to America and the United Kingdom are a factor to be reckoned with. In our own experience, African students in the United Kingdom are fertile soil for propaganda of the nationalist and anti-white type. There can be no doubt that a political section of the community is directing a campaign against the white people and aims at turning them out.

The Commissioners will be aware of the great concessions given in the political field by the establishment of an unofficial and African majority in the Legislative Council. The Commissioners will judge for themselves the fitness of the African to assume such responsibility, and the numbers available with the necessary qualifications for office who would give disinterested service to the state.[35]

In these words Cole attempted not to prejudge the abilities of the newly qualified Africans becoming available for governmental service. There is a hint of criticism for the nationalist movements which he judged would be turning the Europeans out. UAC was, in fact, going along with the Africanization efforts and had in the late thirties begun to train Ghanaians for managerial positions.[36]

Regarding economic causes, Cole asserted that the company itself was best qualified to speak, because of its long experience in trading. He then enumerated the economic issues ascribed to the disorders:[37] high prices, including middlemen's profits and storekeepers' prices; the boycott; conditional sales of goods; a "chit system", which means giving priority of supplies to a person bearing a letter from a influential person;[38] the misrepresentation of reasons for the tortoise pace of "Africanisation"; abuses in the campaign to stop swollen-shoot disease; the level of wages and the evils arising from "retrospective" payments of wages; propaganda on the lack of industrialization; and propaganda on the failure to encourage the investment of African capital.

Cole described the role of UAC in each of these areas, mentioning the close government regulations of prices and the efforts of the company to abide by the regulations. He went on to note that the traditional distribution system was mainly through the middlemen and the small traders who bought from UAC but who were not supervised or policed and whose prices thus did not conform to governmental regulations. He also noted that the press helped to rally sentiment against the European distributors when, in many instances, they were not to blame. Cole's recommendations for changes centered on methods of reducing prices and increasing supplies, changes in distribution, and efforts to have more accurate press reporting.[39] Among the social causes for discontent in the Gold Coast, which according to Cole favored disorderliness, were the grievances of ex-servicemen; the limited number of clerical jobs available for young persons with a very low standard of education;

the lack of widespread and efficient medical services in keeping with the incomes of the people; the absence of a reliable press; calling to the attention of those with limited understanding strikes, disorders, and violence in other parts of the world, principally through the radio; poor liaison between the government and the merchants and the public; high rents; and the positions of the chiefs.[40]

Implicit in the discussion of each of these social causes was a recommendation by George Cole of additional governmental activity in education, housing, and medical services. He also said that the government and the merchants had failed to work closely enough together throughout the postwar period to avoid some of the problems now evident in the Gold Coast. He thus implied that such cooperation should take place.[41]

The UAC testimony presented by Cole was echoed in the Commission's view of the causes of the rioting:[42] The Commission also reported the causes under three major categories—political, economic, and social. Major political causes included: the contacts of a large number of African soldiers with other people, a feeling of political frustration among the educated Africans "who regarded the 1946 Constitution as mere window-dressing"; a failure of the government to realize that increasing literacy brought the Gold Coast into closer contact with political development in other parts of the world; a feeling that "Africanisation was merely a promise"; and a general suspicion of government measures "reinforced by a hostile press" and "heightened by the general failure of the Administration in the field of Public Relations." The last point, which was not covered by UAC testimony dealt with "increasing resentment at the growing concentration of certain trades in the hands of foreigners, particularly at the increase in the number of Syrian merchants."[43] Under economic causes came the government's neutrality in the dispute about high prices; the continuance of wartime control of imports and the shortages of goods; the alleged unfair allocation of goods by the importing firms; the government's acceptance of cutting out diseased trees as the only cure for swollen-shoot disease of cocoa; the limitation on farmers' representatives in control of the Cocoa Marketing Board's reserve funds; and the feeling that the government had not formulated plans for future industrial and agricultural development.[44]

The Commission went on to discuss the social causes, which included an alleged slow development of educational facilities; a shortage of housing; a fear of wholesale alienation of tribal lands; and inadequate legal powers of the government "to deal with speeches designed to arouse disorder and violence."[45] The Commission report stated that His Majesty's Government had the moral obligation of remaining until "the literate population has by experience reached a stage when selfish exploitation is no longer the dominant motive of political power or some corresponding degree of cultural, political and economic achievement has been attained by all three areas now part of the Gold Coast."[46]

To help achieve this goal, the Commission made many recommendations, including provisions for more government responsibility for Africans:

We are satisfied that in the conditions existing today in the Gold Coast a substantial measure of constitutional reform is necessary to meet the legitimate aspirations of the indigenous population. The fact that the three areas—the Colony, Ashanti and the Northern Territories—present, in some aspects, different problems by reason of the varying stages of cultural, political and economic development at which each has arrived, does not in our view provide a valid excuse for delay.

The new Construction ushered in with such promise in 1946 was no doubt well intentioned. Its weakness in our view lay in its conception. It was obviously conceived in the light of pre-war conditions.[47]

In addition, the Commission made specific recommendations for the realization of the ultimate goal of "Africanisation" and self-government in the local authorities, regional councils, town councils, assembly, executive council, and the government.[48]

The Commission also considered various other problems facing the people of the Gold Coast: press relations, immigration, short supplies, high prices, distribution of goods, trading decisions, cocoa marketing, broad cutting-out of cocoa trees, industrial and agricultural bribery, education, labor, housing, and tax reforms.

In regard to pricing and reorganization of the selling system on the Coast, the Commission recommended cooperatives and a more specialized retail trade. It emphasized in conclusion that the whole selling system needed re-organization including an increased number of African organizations in the import trade and increased specialization within, and a more firmly established retail trade throughout the country.[49]

From 1939 onward, the firms had been discussing with the colonial secretary trade abuses, particularly with regard to cocoa marketing and various arrangements, including cooperatives, to avoid these abuses.[50] They did not react one way or the other to the recommendations on market boards or cooperatives. They had already accepted local controls over prices and cocoa marketing through price controls and the Cocoa Marketing Board.

For cocoa marketing, the recommendations centered around the use of the Marketing Board's reserve fund, not only for stabilization of prices but also for the establishment of a cocoa bank to assist the firms. The firms, according to Cole, viewed the protection of the farmers as a primary concern, yet considered the Cocoa Marketing Board to be well constituted. They were anxious to find a way to assure the farmer that the Board's reserves be used to stabilize prices in lean years, as well as be available for his general benefit.[51]

The manufacturing firms, especially Cadburys, continued to support all measures to improve the quality of cocoa and continued as a driving force in efforts to control swollen shoot disease.[52] As buying agents for the Cocoa Marketing Board, the other firms did not then react to the establishment of the Board. They made no comments within six months about the organization nor about distribution of cocoa.

In addition to Commission recommendations for industrialization,[53] there were five problem areas mentioned in agriculture:

(a) The absence of any alternative crops to cocoa.
(b) The lack of close contact between the Department and the farmer.
(c) The weakness of agricultural education, experimentation and demonstration.
(d) The excessive attention to the problems of export crops in comparison with crops for home consumption.
(e) The absence of plans for future development.[54]

George Cole presented the general position of UAC regarding the introduction of industries in the Gold Coast: "The company desires to see the establishment of an industry in any field in which such an industry would be economically sound, and would be able, either to export its products under competitive conditions with the remainder of the world or to market them locally without putting up the price unduly." He goes on to point out ventures that were uneconomical, like palm oil, and profitable undertakings, like the African Timber and Plywood Company and the West African Aluminium Company. Finally, he stated that the main reason that African capital had not come forward for such ventures was the lack of understanding by the African about the normal return on capital invested in such projects and the mistrust Africans had for one another.[55]

The Commission noted the contrast with wartime emphasis:

By way of contrast with the apathy towards food crops, we were told of the war-time agricultural developments, when a phenomenal increase in vegetable production and the development of a bacon industry were quickly achieved to meet the requirements of the Services. We agree that this indicates that results can be achieved under pressure.[56]

Recommendations were also made for the development of trade unions and more employment apprentices, along with more facilities for housing and education. A section on law reforms considered problems of land tenure, sedition, prisoners on remand, and native courts.[57] The Commission report, as did George Cole, listed a number of economic, social and political factors that contributed to the disturbances. Neither Cole's testimony nor the Commission report indicated the priorities of these factors in the situations leading to the disturbances. Certainly the Report indicated the factors contributing to the immediate disturbances or leading to the unrest— factors that spurred people into action, such as prices and lack of supplies, and turning ex-servicemen from the route that many had wished to take to the Castle.

George Cole's testimony indicated that there needed to be closer cooperation between government and business on solutions for the problems of distribution and supply on the Coast. In addition, both the Commission report and Cole agreed that changes in the political system were needed. The Report emphasized this need and called for a detailed study of the position, which would include more participation for the Gold Coast people. Both Cole and the Commission agreed that changes had to be made in the distribution system.[58] The report indicated that a great deal more should be done to involve the Africans in the service industries and in commercial activities.

The Firms, the Colonial Office, and the Government

Between 1939 and 1947 the European firms involved in the cocoa trade had worked closely with the British government and the Gold Coast government, purchasing cocoa from the farmers and selling it to the produce boards. In addition, the firms had expressed their views to the Colonial Office on proposals to establish a marketing board for cocoa on the Coast after the war.

With the establishment of the Marketing Board, for which the firms became licensed buyers, business contacts with the colonial office ceased. There was, furthermore, during the crises of 1947-48, little evidence of the firms making presentations to the Colonial Office in London. Most, if not all, communications were between the firms and the Gold Coast government and/or the Commission of Enquiry. In fact, the London representative of UAC testified only to the Commission in Accra. There were no testimonies taken in London.

By 1948 the Colonial Office, then under the Labour Government, was inclining toward self-government for the colonies, so that the problems of the colony were being handled almost exclusively in the Coast.

The Firms and Development

Public expressions of hostility toward the British firms reached their height in the Gold Coast by 1947. The newspapers and private local firms gave vent to the peoples' concern about the shortage of goods and the increasing prices of these goods, as well as to the difficulties of small business developing exports with the expatriate firms controlling such a large portion of the market. UAC received the greatest proportion of this criticism among the British firms because it both purchased cocoa and supplied goods to the Coast. In addition, it was among the largest of the concerns with long term associations on the Coast. AWAM came in for almost an equal amount of criticism, mainly because it had recommended quotas during the war. UAC, as we see from their communications and from the testimony to the Watson Commision (1948 Commission of Enquiry on the Disturbances) explained the difficulties it faced with postwar shortages and its attempts to keep their goods off the black market. Their emphasis on realizing profits still seemed to include serving the market rather than exploiting it. The firms went along with local controls on the coast through the Cocoa Marketing Board. They continued to serve in the Coast as buying agents for the cocoa marketing board under the conditions established by the Board. The firms thus did not hinder localization of political and economic controls in the Coast government, but by 1947 were accepting this step as necessary in a number of activities.

The Commission report indicated that decisions had to be reached within the territorial areas of the country. Even though the metropolitan government had directed some of the colonial service's activities before and during World War Two, these directives were usually stated in general terms, and were implemented according to local administrative interpretations. Hence the Commission's recommendations were merely to enlarge the scope of participation so as to include local inhabitants in decisions about, and administration of, affairs relating to the Coast.

The Cole testimony was the major new contribution on Coastal trade arising from British business during the disturbances of 1947-48. This testimony afforded the political historian with a view of British business, dominated by a mixture of profit-seeking and enlightened attitude, toward the need for local developments. Again we have a specimen of business motivation which interwove features of profit-seeking and innovation. Cole was speaking in terms of business profits when he mentioned that the firm was reducing the profit margin from 75 percent to 50 percent.[59] The innovative features of UAC's postwar activities on the Coast include the firm's increased training programs and their provisions for indigenous personnel among the managerial staff.[60]

6

THE INDEPENDENCE ROUTE:
1. AFRICANISATION

The activities in the Gold Coast during and after the war accelerated the recruitment of Ghanaians for positions in the Coastal administration and in business management. Before the 1920's some European firms in the Coast had engaged managers from the locality to operate their stores in the outlying areas. By the thirties, however most local managers had been replaced by Europeans often because of irregularities in operations discovered by the firms. ("Europeans" and "Expatriates" are terms used in the Coast for personnel who came from European or British firms or from European countries.) Yet in the mid-twenties, at the time when business was turning away from African managers, Governor Gordon Guggisberg introduced a plan for "increasing the number of Africans holding European appointments [in the government] from 27 to a total of 231" over a period of twenty years.[1] By 1946, however, the number of Africans had increased only to 89, a number far short of the 231 urged by Guggisberg. In the government's statement about the program in 1954, one of the major reasons put forth for the slow increase was the lack of provisions for training Africans for such appointments.[2]

Successive governors changed the emphasis of the program. Thus the next major step after the announcement of the Guggisberg plan was a 1941 survey of departments to ascertain the grades that should be filled by Africans in the next twenty years and to determine the qualifications for African candidates in each grade. Only seven of the government departments were surveyed, including the police, public works, and railway departments. Two major recommendations arising from the report, which was issued in 1944, were that a substantial scholarship program should be launched and the Africanisation policy should give preference to Africans rather than overseas officers for appointments to the Senior Service.[3] These recommendations were implemented first through the creation during the next year of a scholarship selection board to centralize the government's training program and through the establishment in

1948 of an interim Public Service Commissioner—which was followed by a statutory commission in 1950—to ensure that all suitable and qualified African candidates received preference over expatriate recruits. A Commissioner for Africanisation was first appointed in 1950 as an executive officer of the Public Service Commision to ensure that the maximum number of qualified African candidates became available for appointments. The duties of this commissioner were soon turned over to a director of recruitment and training. The Government adopted a recruitment policy in 1952 in the sessional paper no. 3. The Africanisation policy was enunciated and procedures for appointments and promotions in the Civil Service were described in paragraph 105. The policy was:

That when a vacancy occurs in any post . . . no consideration should be given to the recruitment of an expatriate unless and until, after examination of the claims of all Gold Coast African candidates, the Public Service Commission is satisfied that no such qualified and suitable candidate is available.[4]

Nkrumah, as leader of the government, established with the Governor an official party to review the Africanisation program in each grade and department and to recommend new approaches to training and the implementation of the recruitment policies. The working party was also to recommend ways to implement the prime minister's 1953 policy that no further recruitment of overseas officers would be made on pensionable terms. The report of this group that appeared in "A Statement on the Programme of Africanisation of the Public Service". declared that even with expanded facilities for training, including scholarship opportunities sponsored by each department, and the opportunities available at the University College, Kumasi College, the secondary schools, apprenticeship, and technical training programs, a period of three to five years would elapse before suitable candidates would be available in large numbers. Expatriates would still be needed to fill the requirements of the civil service appointments. The statement concluded with a review of the successful efforts towards Africanisation and of the training programs. From 1949 to 1954 the number of Africans holding senior service posts had risen from 171 to 916. Five Africans had been appointed to top level posts since 1952, increasing the number of Africans in these positions to forty-five. And another 20,000 members of the service were Africans.[5]

Even in the late forties both government and business officials cautiously discussed Africanisation of the services, perhaps because managerial training programs had just begun in the late thirties, and governmental efforts to Africanise the Civil Services were just being implemented, although directed by the Governor in the twenties. Speculation about Africanisation was cautious, for training programs were certainly not adequate on the Coast despite the earlier efforts. Ghanaians who had been trained had not been long enough in the services to be evaluated. Yet a great deal of progress was made towards Africanisation with the efforts of the late thirties and the war period. Some concerns were in fact returning to the pattern of the early twentieth century, when a few Africans had held managerial posts. Certainly the expatriate firms were willing to train Africans for management, and in these efforts they were revising the nineteenth century concept of the Africans' ability held by some expatriates and missionaries.

The British Firms: Holts

In some respects the Africanisation policies of the British firms and some banks and mining concerns paralleled these of the government. Early sources on Holts' Africanisation policy include a 1938 letter from H. L. Rawlings, the general manager in Liverpool, to Mr. Winter in Accra:

I hope you will always make it clear to our African Staff that, in this Company, there is no bar to the promotion of any African to European posts merely because he is an African. For the posts now filled by Europeans, we must have certain knowledge and qualifications, general knowledge, and the holders must possess a strong sense of responsibility, the qualities of leadership and high personal integrity. The only reason why Africans do not fill some of these posts at present is that we have, so far, not found any to conform to the standards we demand. No one pretends that every European we have sent out has conformed to the standards. When it is found that he does not, the European concerned is dismissed. Those we have retained do, in our opinion, conform to the standards.

Only once in my experience has the African Staff ever thrown up a man who was potentially fitted to occupy a European post, and that was Mr. Vandepuye. He was advanced by stages to considerable reponsibility. Unfortunately, he failed to take advantage of the opportunity presented to him and disappointed us.[6]

Mr. Rawlings' description of the standards for top positions in the firm reflects the position of most firms' personnel on the Coast in the late thirties. His illustration of Mr. Vandepuye does point out that some Africans on the Coast were qualified for such positions at the time, and that the firm was interested in training such individuals for these positions. These remarks about qualified Africans in the thirties were similar to reviews of Africanisation in the civil service for this period mentioned above. They also reflected attitudes that made it difficult for Africans, or for that matter any "new" groups, to achieve top positions.[6]

In 1940 the Holts general manager reiterated the firm's principles in regard to staff administration and its intention of including the African clerical staff among the pensionable services:

The principals of staff administration, so far as the African Clerical Staff is concerned, do not differ from those in regard to the European Staff. That staff is a permanent pensionable service, which means that, subject to good conduct, industry, mental and physical health, its members have security of employment so long as the Company's revenues enable them to be employed. The African clerical service is not, as yet, a pensionable one. But, it is the Board's hope that, before long it may become so, and, in the meantime, the Board desires it to be administered as though it were already so.

When the war is over and we have to re-expand, we shall need our established African staff very badly. They are the N.C.O.s of the service with all the value and importance implied in that. We shall have a much larger proportion of untrained and semi-trained junior Europeans, and the importance of an experienced African clerical staff in such circumstances is self-evident.

Accordingly, there should be no dismissals on retrenchment grounds of any African clerk of more than 10 years service, without our specific approval. That approval will not be forthcoming unless it is shown that a man has given grounds for dismissal which, in peace times, would be regarded as good grounds. [7]

The European firms were training some Ghanaians for managerial positions as the Second World War began, and in 1945 the Holts records mentioned African managers in the Costal Administration. Some advantages were, according to one report, the Africans' ability to converse in native tongues and their already developed adaptability to the climate. Some disadvantages could be the Ghanaian's untrained business sense and his difficulties in communicating with Europeans:

For some years now we have been experimenting with the appointment of Africans to superior posts in the Coast organisation with a view to their eventual promotion to positions hitherto held by junior Europeans. Apart from the necessity to recognise the growing claims of Africans to positions of responsibility, there are sound business reasons which prompt this policy. Junior Europeans are likely to be unconscionably expensive after the war and, in the competitive days ahead, will prove a severe drain on the Company's limited profits.

The African understands the mentality of his compatriot far better than a European can hope to do and can converse with him freely in his own language. Moreover, an African will not expect the long periods of recuperative leave which are necessary for the European and will therefore ensure a much desired continuity in any post to which he is appointed.

There are, of course, many drawbacks. The African lacks the background from which the average European has benefited, and his sense of ethics is far less highly developed. He has a relatively quick brain which enables him to acquire knowledge, but often lacks the understanding to absorb it and, still more, the initiative to apply it. In his contacts with Europeans he has to employ a language other than his own and his ability to express himself in English suffers from faults of verbosity and exaggeration. In short, he possesses the intelligence but too often lacks the integrity, understanding, initiative and sense of responsibility which make for the successful agent.

In the Gold Coast, despite many disappointments and set-backs, some success has attended our efforts to initiate Africans to positions of increased responsibility. Achimota College provides a wider field for advanced education than any comparable institution to be found in other British West African colonies and is less of a forcing house than the higher educational establishments in Nigeria. The Gold Coast, moreover by virtue of its relatively greater prosperity over a fairly extended period, has felt the impact of Western civilisation to a more profound extent than its less advanced neighbours and is beginning to "think" European. Despite this, serious defects of character have manifested themselves in many of the Gold Coast trainees.[8]

These three communications constitute a good review of the transition taking place in the thinking of business and government about the involvement of Ghanaians. Philip Curtin has examined in details such views about African ethics. The people of the Gold Coast, as the last report indicated, had for some years and for a longer period than any other African people participated in European educational systems and had begun to adopt some European modes of activity. They were already in clerical positions during the thirties and with the war were being placed in some managerial positions. Still, in 1945 and even in 1948 most expatriates in government and business thought that though the Gold Coasters would gradually take over in economic and governmental affairs, the training period would require several decades. Not even the advisers to the governor thought, in 1948, that independence could be achieved within ten years.[9] Any discussion in the early forties of African managerial staff was written in cautious terms and with some hesitancy, because, though a few Gold Coasters had demonstrated considerable ability, many were not yet trained or had not been involved before such economic and governmental activities, and thus were untried and unknown quantities. These discussions in the 1940's, when contrasted with those of expatriates and missionaries during the 1870's and 1880's, demonstrated comparatively greater confidence in the Gold Coasters' abilities.[10]

Holts had been in the Coast for only twelve years but had frequently, in their administrative communications, demonstrated concern about African staff and managers. The company's first report on this matter, however, emerged only after the disturbances, and at the same time that Africanisation was being reemphasized by the government and the other companies.

Significantly, the company's report on managerial staff policy in December of 1948 mentioned Holts' efforts toward Africanisation and its parallels with the government policy:

During the last few years, the policy of this company in regard to the promotion and recruitment of suitable Africans to the Managerial grades within the Coast Establishment has been clearly laid down.

It should be emphasised to all members of our African Staff that there is just as promising a future for educated Africans in the realm of commerce, as there is in Government service, and that steps have been taken to make that service, as far as this Company is concerned, equal to any career which is open to them.

They should realise that it is entirely up to each one of them to show, by diligence and hard work, and by identifying themselves with the interests of this Company in West Africa, that they are worthy of promotion to the Managerial grades.

In the future, the Managerial grade, comprising African Assistants and African Agents (Cadets are not to be considered as within the Managerial sphere but as a direct lead thereto) will enjoy all the privileges extended to their European counterparts. A difference in rates of remuneration, necessitated by expatriation considerations in the case of the European, and certain facilities given to Europeans under that heading such as housing, free medical attention and drugs, will continue to be confined to Managerial Staff recruited from European sources. Apart from those expatriation provisions, however, the treatment of Africans posted or promoted to the Managerial grades, will be exactly as laid down for their European colleagues.[11]

The expatriation privileges mentioned were similar to those extended to all Europeans in government or business and also included, as mentioned earlier, recuperative leaves. Africans received different housing and medical benefits. Europeans coming to the tropical climates of Africa found adjustment quite difficult and were given leaves every few years. The Nkrumah government in 1954 recognized the necessity of giving these special privileges to the expatriates until such time as sufficient numbers of Africans were trained for the positions.[12] The Africans were therefore still being discriminated against.

The Holts report continued by indicating that the company would no longer refer to "African" agents or assistants, but would include these positions in the "Managerial Staff". The procedures outlined in the report were to be adopted on January 1st, 1949.[13] Another communication to district agents in West Africa sent out that same month noted some difficulties in finding African personnel to fill the positions.

Some District Agents have told us, from time to time, that they are having difficulty in obtaining learners and cadets with suitable educational qualifications and of the right type; and that the best of the products of Yaba, Achimota, and King's College Lagos, are going into Government Service. If our policy in regard to the appointment of Africans to the Managerial grades is to bear fruit, it is essential that our service should be no less attractive than the Colonial Governments. Furthermore, the members of the African Staff already holding appointments in the Managerial grades must have clear evidence that they will be paid salaries commensurate with the additional reponsibility which they will have to undertake and, although very few of the staff have reached the upper limit of the scales in which they are placed, we want them to know beyond doubt that outstanding ability, integrity, and ability to accept responsibility will be justly rewarded irrespective of race and colour.

Africans can qualify for appointments in the Managerial Grades in two ways. Men with Yaba, Achimota or similar qualifications can be engaged as Cadets and, subject to their making satisfactory progress and being suitable from the point of view of character, they become eligible for promotion to the Assistant Grade after serving a probationary period, which is usually about three years.

Members of the African clerical staff of outstanding ability and character can also be promoted to the grade of Assistant, but, in their cases, such promotions must usually be made before a man is 35 years of age. Older men are, as a general rule, not capable of acquiring the Managerial outlook: they have been trained as Clerks and a good Clerk is unlikely to make a successful Manager if he has not been trained to think things out for himself during his early service with the Company.

It has already been recognised by the Colonial Governments that the same basic rate of salary shall be paid to Africans and Europeans holding similar appointments, but Europeans receive expatriation pay roughly equivalent to one-third of the basic salary. All of you will fully understand the principle whereby expatriation pay is paid to non-natives: and the time has come for us to revise our scales of pay as far as the Managerial Grades are concerned, with that principle in our minds.[14]

Although Holts had made some efforts to train personnel during the war years, not until 1952 did this training become a part of Holts program.[15] For a four-year period after 1953 the Company recorded an average of four African agents, one to two assistants, and four to five clerical assistants. The employment of Ghanaians in all facets of the business operations was becoming a reality by the time of independence.[16]

The British Firms: UAC

UAC's policy of including Africans can be traced back to 1926, when two Africans on the Coast served as managers of stores. Some training began in the late thirties. J. O. T. Agyeman, who was one of the first Africans to join the company and to benefit from the training opportunities, became, during the sixties, manager of the Ghana National Trading Corporation.

Among the expatriates to remain was Sir Patrick FitzGerald—as an adviser to the GNTC management, however, rather than with UAC. By 1961 when UAC began reducing its operations in Ghana, the number of Ghanaians in managerial positions and on the UAC staff rose to between seventy and eighty. Courses for prospective managers were continued by UAC despite the decrease in operations in Ghana; in 1966, 208 of the 400 managers were Ghanaian.[17]

Arthur Creech-Jones, who in 1945 became Secretary of State for the Colonies, wrote from the House of Commons during the forties, probably after his visit to West Africa, to Mr. Mellor of UAC, urging UAC to take a number of steps to bring a healthier feeling on the coast toward UAC.[18] Among the actions suggested was assistance with scholarships and technical institutes. No mention was made of increasing the number of Africa managerial position:

Scholarships to this country, technical institutes, wings to university institutions, more science laboratories, teacher training colleges, and many other things may be matters for the Colonial Government, but both the people and the Colonial Governments with the existing limited resources, make financial provisions near to impossible. Yet much wealth goes overseas and there seems a conspiracy to compel the colonial people to live on the lowest possible margins. Big business could help.[19]

Although the major impetus for Africanisation in UAC occurred in 1949, preludes to such efforts may be seen in a statement on revisions of salaries and wages for African personnel and in the remarks of George Cole (now Lord Cole) on Africanisation in testimony to the 1948 Commission on the Disturbances. The salaries revision letter went out in 1947 from London to major sections of the company in West Africa and indicated:

It has been decided . . . in pursuance of the Company's policy to offer attractive careers to suitable Africans in the Company's service, to revise the Company's salary scales in order to bring them up to date.

This letter is to advise you of the suggested new scales for clerical staff which have been evolved after careful study and full discussion in London, with the General Managers' recommendations before us.

This examination led to the conclusion that it is possible for the Company to adopt uniform scales throughout British West Africa. In our view this course has many desirable features and it follows the recommendations made to Government in the Harragin Report.[20]

In putting forward the scales below, full consideration was given to the individual recommendations of General Managers and it is felt that in every case any modification now put forward is so slight that each General Manager will readily fall in with proposals, so that uniformity can be achieved.[21]

The first mention of African personnel in George Cole's 1948 testimony on the disturbances involved the African retail storekeepers to whom UAC sold goods and the allegations that "their men, employees of the Company, have taken advantage of their remoteness from continuous and immediate control, to demand prices in excess of those fixed by the Company".[22] Despite the possible truth of these allegations, during the disturbances the company supported in the same document a policy of Africanisation of personnel:

The United Africa Company's policy has been progressive. The whole trend of our policy has been to maintain unchanged our position in the commercial life of the Colony but gradually to hand over to Africans the work for which they are suited as they become capable of it, while ourselves introducing and maintaining skills which are at present beyond them. The United Africa Company is probably well ahead of all other concerns in the promotion of Africans, but the way has not been easy and there have been experiences which might well have discouraged us. In 1939 there were 30 Africans of Managerial status in the group. At December, 1947, there were 68. This was not the result of war, but the development of a policy promoting to management the indigenous people of the country in which the business operates. Several years before the war the foundation of the policy was laid down and it has been carefully developed and closely supervised, both locally and from London. A special system of appointment and training for such Africans has been laid down and an endeavour made to attract the best material from the schools. On appointment an African Manager receives a salary of £350 per annum (a European on appointment is on £500 p.a. plus quarters and medical attention). On January 1st, 1944, a Pension Fund for all African staff and a Gratuity Scheme for unskilled labour was introduced.[23]

Cole thus outlined UAC achievements toward Africanisation of its managerial staff with mention of a policy already started before the Second World War and noting the doubling of this staff by 1947. The salary and benefits of African managers seemed consistent with both governmental and other commercial firms' practices.

Cole went on to illustrate some of the difficulties that the firm had in giving Africans positions of responsibility in the company. They were similar to the difficulties noted by the Holts general manager.

That there is agitation for more Africanisation generally is understandable; but it is difficult to believe that those with the loudest voices do not well know the difficulties of the problem and limitations and inadequacies of the available material. For many years we have been doing our utmost to discover suitable African material for training to the higher posts of management. The results are disappointing to those who expect that fundamental changes in character can be brought about in a few years. Africans have risen to very responsible positions, but none of them has ever shown the capacity of challenge for the post of General Manager or anything approaching it. Perhaps the greatest difficulty facing the most ardent advocate of Africanisation is getting African staff to cooperate whole-heartedly with African Managers. They often distrust them, sometimes oppose them and have been known to do everything possible to bring them down. Again, tribal customs place an enormous strain on any African so promoted, and there are extremely few who find it possible to resist the family and other calls made upon them the moment they achieve a position of authority.[24]

By these remarks Cole has described the difficulties any group—ethnic or national, or, for that matter, women—faces upon entering a new professional activity in any field and in any country. The candidate has to have the cooperation of his peers and followers, as implied by Cole, but in addition the person must have the backing of his superiors and their confidence in his ability to rise, a point seemingly not realized in this description of Cole's but acceded to in part in his next statement about some of the Africans placed in managerial positions:

The Company's staff sees so many Africans in real positions of management that they have no doubt of the genuineness of the Company's intentions. Nothing has given the Company greater and better founded confidence in this matter than the outstanding loyalty to the Company displayed recently [during the 1948 disturbances] by its African staff in particularly trying and in many cases exceedingly dangerous circumstances, when they have, at the risk of unpopularity and physical violence, stood by and protected members of our European staff, and often with no European there to prompt, have saved by their personal action, the Company's buildings and stocks from the hands of their riotous fellow countrymen.[25]

A favorable report of the UAC Africanisation policy was given by Colin Legum, a well-known reporter on African affairs, in a 1958 seminar on West Africa:

All the major firms operating in West Africa had shown remarkable political foresight and adaptability with regard to the changing situation—despite the extreme delicacy with which they had to walk. UAC in particular had since 1949 been pursuing a steady policy of Africanisation with extensive schemes for the training of African staff—despite the steady drain of staff so trained to run their own businesses.[26]

Between 1949 and 1957 the number of Ghanaians included in UAC management doubled from 59 to 120 (see Tables 1 and 2). This increase was a steady one of around four Africans per year until 1955, when 14 additional Ghanaians were added, 13 in 1956, and 20 in 1957—the year of independence. The percentage of Ghanaians among the management staff remained around 18 from 1950 to 1954. From 1955, when the percentage increased to 21, the numbers of Ghanaians on the staff steadily increased to 25 percent in 1957, 39.6 percent in 1962, and 47 percent in 1964. UAC published its Africanisation figures consistently during this period, while the other firms were not as consistent about publication on Africanisation until independence. (See also Table 6.)

According to Ghanaians who had been associated with UAC (or firms preceding UAC), these firms had a few Africans in managerial positions in the twenties. Yet a vigorous policy of Africanisation was not initiated until the late thirties by UAC (which had been formed on the Coast in 1930). The first UAC African manager of this period was in Kumasi in 1935.[27]

Cadburys

Cadburys contributed to Africanisation on the Coast in two significant ways: through scholarships and through employment of Africans. The firm was a pioneer among the European concerns in making scholarships available for Africans in the Gold Coast. A grant was first made in 1926 to Achimota College for scholarships in agriculture for both men and women students. In 1949 the Cadbury Scholarship Funds amounted to £20,000. That same year the colonial

Table 1. UAC MANAGEMENT 1949-1964 AFRICAN AND EUROPEAN MEMBERS

Year	Territory	Africans		Europeans		Total
		No.	%	No.	%	%
1949	The Gambia	2		15		
	Sierra Leone	3		31		
	Gold Coast	59	20.6	227	79.4	286
	Nigeria	50		532		
	Total	114		805		
1950	The Gambia	2		19		
	Sierra Leone	5		32		
	Gold Coast	58	18.6	253	81.4	311
	Nigeria	54		536		
	Total	119		840		
1951	The Gambia	2		19		
	Sierra Leone	6		37		
	Gold Coast	63	17.7	292	82.3	355
	Nigeria	59		575		
	Total	130		923		
1952	The Gambia	2		20		
	Sierra Leone	6		38		
	Gold Coast	66	17	321	83	387
	Nigeria	79		286		
	Total	153		992		
1953	The Gambia	2		20		22
	Sierra Leone	6		40		46
	Ghana	72	18.3	322	81.7	394
	Nigeria	80		627		697
	Total	160		999		1,159
1954	The Gambia	2		19		21
	Sierra Leone	7		44		51
	Ghana	73	18.2	329	81.8	402
	Nigeria	83		652		735
	Total	165		1,044		1,209
1955	The Gambia	2		19		21
	Sierra Leone	11		43		54
	Ghana	87	21	327	79	414
	Nigeria	99		676		775
	Total	199		1,065		1,264

Table 1 continued

Year	Territory	Africans No.	%	Europeans No.	%	Total %
1956	The Gambia	3		15		18
	Sierra Leone	16		44		60
	Ghana	100	21.6	362	78.4	462
	Nigeria	119		732		851
	Total	238		1,153		1,391
1957[c]	The Gambia	3		15		18
	Sierra Leone	25		44		69
	Ghana	120	25	360	75	480
	Nigeria	156		740		896
	Total	304		1,159		1,463
1958[d]	The Gambia					
	Sierra Leone					
	Ghana					
	Nigeria					
	Total					
1962	The Gambia	6		9		15
	Sierra Leone	23		48		71
	Ghana	174	39.6	265	60.4	439
	Nigeria	273		619		892
	Total	476		941		1,417
1963	The Gambia	7		6		13
	Sierra Leone	22		46		68
	Ghana	164	41.5	231	58.5	395
	Nigeria	303		531		834
	Total	496		814		1,310
1964	The Gambia	8		6		14
	Sierra Leone	18		40		58
	Ghana	173	47.4	192	52.6	365
	Nigeria	328		466		794
	Total	527		704		1,231

[a] Tables on European and African staff for UAC appear in UAC, *Statistical and Economic Review*, 12 (September 1953), 38–41; 20 (September 1957), 39; and 30 (September 1965), 57.
[b] Percentage of Africans among the total managerial staff in the Gold Coast.
[c] The figures are given for mid-year during 1957 only.
[d] Statistics were not available from 1958 to 1961.

secretary suggested that these funds be transferred, for administrative purposes, from Crown agents to the Achimota School. By 1951 the funds were vested in trust under the care of the principal of Achimota.[28]

In addition to scholarships, Cadburys made provision during the thirties and forties for the construction and equipment of some educational facilities and a number of community halls.[29] Cadbury Hall was connected with a training program at the Agricultural Training Centre in Kumasi. In the first year at the Centre, a student received his basic education at Cadbury Hall; in the second year, practical experience was available at an agricultural station; and during the third year, second-division officers were trained at Cadbury Hall. The students held Cambridge School certificates or primary school leaving certificates, or had served as field assistants.[30]

Less emphasis was placed, in Cadburys' reports, on Africanisation efforts than a scholarship and education endeavors. There were scattered mentions of African staff members. In the 1943-44 season report, for example, it was stated that "one further African member was added to the staff of supervisors—another . . . resigned . . . to come to England to study law".[31] In the 1946-47 report, African staff was discussed in two sections. The first related to the defalcation of two clerks and the other discussed the fact that "for the first time in several years the company had a full European Staff in operation", while expressing promise for all the African supervisors. Those Africans recommended for admission to the Pension Fund included one who was training as general manager secretary, another as a transport clerk, and the third as a supervisor.[32] The general manager's report stated:

With the exception of those concerned in irregularities at various Buying Stations, all clerks have worked well. The Yonsoh clerk, it appears, worked in good faith—way outside of class . . .

All the five supervisors in training have done quite well. Yeboah, stationed at Koforidua, had difficult and heart-breaking times . . . not much opportunity to show capabilities.[33]

In the report further mention is made of the eleven Africans who were members of the Pension Fund, and of the sixteen Europeans. At this time there were many African clerks who were not members of the Fund. There was a large African staff of clerks (144), drivers (211), and workmen (807). Cadburys' operations on the Coast were certainly not as extensive as UAC's, and the number of managerial positions were quite limited. In large part the size of staff perhaps explains Cadburys' concentration on training programs and the fact that the company mentioned Africanisation of management only briefly before independence.

The first African appointments to the supervisory staff were in the thirties. The appointments carried management status and in the

Table 2. THE UNITED AFRICA GROUP'S STAFF AND LABOUR FORCE[a] 1949-1956

Year	Territory	Office Organization	Store-keepers and Others	Skilled Labour	Unskilled Labour		Total
					Permanent	Casual (Average)	
1949	The Gambia	50	122	140	245	130	687
	Sierra Leone	287	55	108	516	135	1,101
	Gold Coast	2,328	2,670	1,108	3,508	2,471	12,085
	Nigeria	3,823	1,191	3,571	16,829	7,919	33,333
	Total	6,488	4,038	4,927	21,098	10,655	47,206
1950	The Gambia	54	149	222	268	93	786
	Sierra Leone	327	55	119	537	225	1,263
	Gold Coast	2,457	2,999	1,085	3,678	2,299	12,518
	Nigeria	3,773	1,087	3,419	14,569	6,790	29,638
	Total	6,611	4,290	4,845	19,052	9,407	44,205
1951	The Gambia	66	136	189	280	89	760
	Sierra Leone	421	50	106	644	145	1,366
	Gold Coast	2,947	2,947	1,362	4,065	1,400	12,608
	Nigeria	4,186	1,177	3,550	15,678	5,535	30,126
	Total	7,507	4,310	5,207	20,667	7,169	44,860
1952	The Gambia	76	158	196	271	73	774
	Sierra Leone	436	50	107	639	115	1,347
	Gold Coast	2,945	2,884	1,882	4,605	1,753	14,073
	Nigeria	4,552	1,298	4,327	15,923	3,870	29,970
	Total	8,009	4,390	6,512	21,442	5,811	46,164

Table 2 *continued*

1953	The Gambia	64	145	158	267	58	692
	Sierra Leone	453	48	112	646	151	1,410
	Ghana	2,918	2,748	1,995	4,431	1,611	13,703
	Nigeria	4,501	1,284	4,827	17,235	3,359	31,206
	Total	7,936	4,225	7,092	22,579	5,179	47,011
1954	The Gambia	69	142	134	256	63	664
	Sierra Leone	514	449	125	644	65	1,397
	Ghana	3,033	2,630	2,447	4,393	1,261	13,764
	Nigeria	4,553	1,422	5,078	16,312	4,178	31,543
	Total	8,169	4,243	7,784	21,605	5,567	47,368
1955	The Gambia	72	141	127	299	93	662
	Sierra Leone	508	48	119	666	46	1,387
	Ghana	3,051	2,343	2,285	4,057	1,712	13,448
	Nigeria	4,906	1,618	5,402	15,641	3,777	31,344
	Total	8,537	4,150	7,933	20,593	7,628	46,841
1956	The Gambia	72	113	121	210	54	570
	Sierra Leone	585	67	188	705	214	1,759
	Ghana	3,287	2,146	2,718	4,513	1,748	14,412
	Nigeria	5,433	1,512	5,912	15,403	4,060	32,420
	Total	9,377	3,838	8,939	20,931	6,076	49,161

[a]UAC, *Statistical and Economic Review*, 12 (September 1957), 40; and 20 (September 1957), 41.

early years membership in the Bournville pension scheme. Later a provident fund scheme operated in Ghana for all eligible African staff.[34] Again in 1951 the pension scheme for African employees was considered on a contributory basis.[35] Note was also made of two African supervisors who had visited England.

The first lengthy mention of Africanisation was made immediately before independence in the 1956-57 General Manager's Report:

Before the commencement of next season I hope to make recommendations for the appointment of more supervisors to the rank of Agent. I also propose making several more appointments to the grade of Supervisor-in-training. These latter appointments have generally been for a period of two seasons but it may be necessary for some of these new people to have a longer period although they will be appointed from among the buying clerks.

There seems no doubt that in the new Ghana we should Africanise our staff to the maximum compatible with efficiency: in fact it may be necessary to carry additional staff in the senior African appointments to carry out this policy . . .[36]

Banks and Mines

The firms continued to talk with the new government about Africanisation up to independence in 1957 and afterward as well. There was a need for European technical assistance well into the sixties, and it still remains in some situations today. (Whenever possible, we shall, around the time of independence, refer to the employment of Ghanaians rather than Africanisation, even though the latter term was still used in West Africa.) The Africanisation policies of a number of concerns, including some mines and the banks, were not realized until after independence.

Barclays DCO, one of the main banking operations on the Coast before independence, began a training program for Ghanaians in July 1956. The first trainee is now retired from the Bank's service but continues as a member of the Ghana Board of Directors. In the ten-year period after 1956 eleven Ghanaians were sent to the United Kingdom for special training (for periods of from four months to two years). Between 1956 and 1961, thirty-seven Ghanaians were accepted from other organizations for training in branches of Barclays Bank. Up to 1966 the total number of Ghanaians who had received training in Accra were 1162 and in London, 16. By the same year, as Table 3 demonstrates, half of the managers of the 24 branches in Ghana were Ghanaians.

The Consolidated African Selection Trust (CAST), in its statement about training for positions of responsibility, mentioned that "the need for training Ghanaians at every level of responsibility in the mining industry has long been recognized by 'CAST' ". Before 1957 a variety of training schemes had been in operation under individual departments, but in 1958 the entire program was brought under the

Table 3.
BARCLAYS DCO: GHANAIANS ON STAFF (JANUARY 1966)

(a) Number of messengers employed	(locally recruited)	123
Number of clerical staff	(locally recruited)	605
Number of clerical staff	(British covenated)	57
		785

(b) Number of Ghanaians holding senior positions:
   12 Managers
   1 Sub-Manager
   6 Sub-Managers of sub-branches

(c) Number of offices
   24 Branches
   6 Sub-Branches
   29 Agencies

Source: Letter, July 1966.

Department of Education and Training. In the CAST statement the department was described:

From a humble beginning, the Department has now spread its activities to all aspects of education and training, and in this pamphlet we have attempted to give readers an insight into the aims and objectives of the training schemes and how they fit into the general pattern of the Africanisation policy of Ghana's leading diamond mining Company.[37]

Table 4 gives some indication of the varieties of CAST training for community operations from mining to nursing and the efforts of the company to place Ghanaians in responsible positions. The latter efforts were begun in 1957 with two students who were sent to the United Kingdom to qualify as mining engineers. Ten mining engineers were trained in the UK in Cornwall by 1963 under this program. Two of the engineers have returned to work at CAST and two have been placed with the British National Coal Board.

Little effort was made before 1956 to train Ghanaians for staff positions in CAST, and the greatest efforts were exerted in the mid-sixties. In 1938 approximately 25 Africans served on the staff; in 1954, when a big increase in staff began, there were 40. In December 1958 the staff totaled 92 and there were 5 or 6 Ghanaians in managerial, personnel, and mining positions of responsibility; the rest were in line management. On the senior staff in 1961 there were 86 expatriates and 42 Ghanaians, and in 1963 there were 85 expatriates and 40 Ghanaians. It was expected that by January of 1968 the number of expatriates in the mine would be 50, with Ghanaians numbering 101.[38]

Table 4.

CAST: TRAINING PROGRAMS FOR GHANAIANS 1958-63

Mining school senior staff		
Associateship of the Camborne School of Mines		10
Plant shiftsmen	have taken course	20
	completed	12
	annual expectancy	8-10
National certificate course	have taken course	2
	in progress	1
Artisan and specialist course	have taken course	8
	in progress	10
Nursing course	in progress	14
Accountancy and secretarial course	in progress	14

Apprentices are paid at normal company rates, but contribute toward the cost of their catering.

The first intake of twenty took place in August 1957, and was followed in subsequent years by further intakes.

To date, no less than one hundred and twenty youths have passed through the full-time course, and the majority have found employment in the Company Workshops.

Source: CAST Department of Training and Welfare, Akwatia, Ghana, May 1963, pp. 5-6.

Other indirect benefits to the community provided by CAST in the fifties included employment, housing, hospitals, and education and training schemes. These benefits were described in CAST testimony before the Concession Commission in 1958 as follows:

Apart from the direct benefits in the way of payments of rents, royalties, duty and tax, the landowners and the community at large benefit indirectly in many other ways from the Company's operations. Some of these ways are as follows:

  (a) Employment: Regular employment is available to some 3,000 men and women, many in skilled jobs, due to the high degree of mechanisation now achieved. Rates of pay compare favourably with those elsewhere in Ghana, and additional benefits such as paid leave and retirement gratuities are provided.

  Wages and salaries paid in 1956/57 amounted to a total of £479,773. The figure for 1957/1958 is estimated to be £538,000.

(b) Housing: The Company has at present 1,475 well-built quarters of varying types, in which 52% of its employees are housed. No rents or sanitation or other fees are charged. The cost of maintenance for 1956/57 was £51,625.

Electricity is supplied to some of the more senior type quarters. Piped water is laid on to all camps. There is no charge for these services.

(c) Hospital: The Mine Hospital has 52 beds; a full-time medical officer and nursing sister, and 42 other staff. Treatment is entirely free of charge for both employees and dependents. The cost of medical services in 1956/57 was £17,131.

(d) Education: The Company awards 28 scholarships to primary, middle and secondary schools in Ghana. Also 3 scholarships for 3/4 years course in the United Kingdom for degrees in mining engineering. Three nurses from the Mine Hospital are studying in England to be state registered nurses. The approximate cost of these scholarships is £3,000 per annum.

A building is provide free of charge at one of the Company's camps for use as a local council school.

(e) Training Schemes: The Company has built a trade training centre at Akwatia at a cost of £17,000. This provides 5 years apprenticeship courses in the mechanical and electrical trades and is open to all Ghanaians. The cost of running is £8,000/£10,000 p.a.

A £25,000 scheme, including the building of a residential hostel, for the training of young Ghanaians in mining techniques to enable them to rise to posts on the senior staff has been approved and will be commenced in June 1958.

(f) Miscellaneous Welfare Facilities for Employees: These include 2 staff clubs, tennis courts, a football field, 3 staff retail stores, a radio rediffusion service (free), cinema shows (free) and an infant welfare clinic.[39]

The Chamber of Mines began a training program for miners during the late forties. The program was not extended to managerial positions until the sixties. Many of the trained personnel went on to positions in the Ashanti Goldfields,[40] which has some training programs for Ghanaians but relied upon the Chamber of Mines until the mid-sixties (see Table 5).[41]

Governmental Policy and the European Firms

Even though the three British firms before World War II had made some efforts at training and employment of Africans, none of these firms announced Africanisation policies until the late forties, several years after wartime conditions had brought a curtailment of operations or the shortage of technical expatriate manpower on the Coast. The firms had made some efforts to bring Africans into management before the war, but concerted efforts were certainly not apparent until the late forties and early fifties. UAC, according to George Cole's testimony in 1948, had started a program of Africanisation in the thirties and the African portion of the staff had doubled by 1947.[42] These policies of Africanisation seem to have been spurred by the 1948 disturbances when business, on the one

Table 5. ASHANTI GOLDFIELDS EXPATRIATES AND
GHANAIAN PERSONNEL BY DEPARTMENT, 1962-1966

Department	1.10.62		1.10.64		1.10.65		1.4.66	
	Ex.	*Af.*	*Ex.*	*Af.*	*Ex.*	*Af.*	*Ex.*	*Af.*
Underground	62	3	54	13	51	22	47	22
Survey	11	1	8	3	7	3	8	3
Sampling	2	1	2	1	2	1	2	2
Forestry	2	–	4	–	5	1	3	2
Salvage	1	–	—	–	—	–	—	–
Geological & diamond drill	8	1	4	1	4	2	5	2
Assay	2	–	2	–	1	1	1	1
Study, labour control planning	7	–	6	–	6	1	5	2
Engineering	43	3	35	16	36	18	38	19
Mines secretary, welfare, personnel, Ashanti Times	5	3	3	4	2	6	2	6
Accounts	5	4	4	6	2	7	3	7
Stores	3	–	2	3	2	4	3	4
Security	3	1	3	1	3	1	3	1
Medical	1	–	2	2	1	4	2	4
Reduction	23	2	18	8	19	9	20	9
Capital projects	1	–	1	–	—	–	—	–
Canteen	2	–	2	–	2	–	2	–
School	–	–	–	–	1	–	1	–
	181	19	150	58	144	80	145	84
Overall total	200		208		244		229	

Source: Letter from W. M. Jones, Ashanti Goldfields, Obuasi, August 11, 1966.

hand, just after the war was making some efforts to insert expatriates in technical positions, and when the Government, on the other hand, was again, for the third time in the century, forwarding the policy of Africanisation— this time with vigor. (The first governmental effort, it will be recalled, had been in the administration of Guggisberg in the twenties and the second during the administration of Sir Alan Burns in the early forties.) Business efforts to interest expatriates in technical positions soon turned to training programs for Ghanaians (see Table 6).

The banks, as exemplified by Barclay's DCO, and the mines, by CAST and Ashanti Goldfields, began to place emphasis on Africanisation and training programs in the years immediately before independence. The results of these efforts were noticeable in Barclays and CAST by the mid-1960's; they were more limited but still apparent in the Ashanti Goldfields operation by the late sixties. The Chamber of Mines' efforts to train Ghanaian miners brought noticeable results perhaps earlier than the Ashanti operations.

As far as this investigation can detect, there seem to have been no direct communications between the Colonial Office in London and the British firms on the issue of Africanisation, nor were there pressures by the office on the firms in England to use more Ghanaians.[43] Creech-Jones, before coming to the Colonial Office, did suggest to UAC some training efforts, and while he was secretary of state he communicated with Nkrumah about training people for Gold Coast economic development.[44] But there seem to have been few if any communications from the firms to the government on this issue. Perhaps these efforts toward Africanisation are best reflected by C. H. Wilson's description of the firms' attitude toward nonpolitical movements.[45] The firms did not oppose political change, nor did they try to arrest the increased political activity of the Ghanaians. They waited until changes took place and then attempted to cooperate with the new political leaders. Some say that the firms, realizing that both the economic and political situations in West Africa would have to change, continued their own healthy economic status by not actively opposing the new political movements.[46] Among the trading firms, UAC through its predecessors did involve Africans up to the 1920's in district managerial positions. Under the new organization, formed in 1929, the company began in the late thirties to train Africans in management.

The firms contributed in varying degrees, from 1937 to 1957, to the development of the indigenous managerial personnel. Cadburys assisted through scholarships and grants for educational institutions as well as through gradual involvement of Africans in the firm's business on the Coast. UAC began again in the late thirties to train Africans for managerial positions and continued this program gradually, as the statistics in Tables 1 and 6 show. This policy continued after independence. Among the mining concerns, CAST, in the fifties, was considerably involved in recruiting Africans for management. Though Ashanti Goldfields used Africans trained by the Chamber of Mine schools for foremen, a considerable lag occurred during the sixties in the employment of Africans in managerial and top managerial positions.

The war and independence movements in the Gold Coast caused most British businesses to react quickly to the gradual rise of employment expectations among the Coastal people.[47] Africanisation of the firms occurred, along with the involvement of Africans in the civil service. Yet neither government nor business officials thought in the forties that the necessary training for self-government and Africanisation of business or government could be achieved within two decades. Immediately after World War Two, because of

Table 6. COMPARATIVE FIGURES: GHANAIANS IN CIVIL SERVICE AND THE BRITISH FIRMS FROM 1922 (1938) TO 1964 (1968)

	Civil Service[a]				UAC[b]		Cadburys[c]		Holts[d]	CAST[e]	
	No. Africans	% of Total Establishment	Senior Executive Officers[f]	Top Level Africans	No.	%	No.	%		No.	%
1922	27										
1938										25	
1939					30						
1946	89										
1947					68						
1948											
1949	171	10.3	32		59	21					
1950	268	13.5	72		58	19					
1951	351	16.1	89		63	18					
1952	520	20.4	118	40	66	18	11	41			
1953	751	19.3	187		72	18			average 1953–57		
1954	916	35.8	180	45	73	19				92 Africans, with 5 or 6 in managerial positions	
	(20,000 members of service)										
1955					87	21			4 agents 4 clerical assistants		
1956					100	22					
1957					120	25					
1958											
1959											
1960											
1961					70					42 Ghanaians	33

Table 6 *continued*

Year			
1962	174	40	40 Ghanaians 32
1963	164	42	
1964	173	47	
1965			
1966	208	52	101 Ghanaians 67
1967			
1968			

[a] Africanisation figures 1949-54, in Gold Coast, *A Statement on the Programme of the Africanisation of the Public Service* (Accra: Government Printing Department, 1954), Appendix 1, p. 2.
[b] See Tables 1 and 2 and pp. 75-84.
[c] Cadburys, see pp. 78-84.
[d] Holts, see pp. 71-75
[e] CAST, see pp. 86-87.
[f] Africans.

the lack of educational facilities, only a few Ghanaians were trained technically on the Coast. Only after independence were the technical training and university facilities significantly expanded in Ghana. Before then, Ghanaians usually had gone to Europe or the United States for such training.

UAC had the largest operation on the Coast, and was among the first of the firms to offer training for management. Cadburys had only a few managerial positions on the Coast, and concentrated its efforts on improvements in education facilities for Gold Coasters. Holts began its operations on the Coast in the late thirties and was withdrawing from some of its coastal activities by the fifties.

According to the government's and the firms' records (Table 6), Africanisation was occurring at about the same pace in each operation. The civil service and UAC have maintained the most complete records, which indicate similar percentages of Africans in the establishment—in 1949, 10 percent in the civil service and 20 percent in UAC. The civil service percentage had increased to 20 in 1952, while the UAC figure was 17 percent for that year. The UAC percentage rose to 21 percent in 1955, however, and 25 percent in 1957. After independence the percentage of Ghanaians in management reached 40 in 1962 and 52 in 1966. CAST began its Africanisation program in the fifties reporting 5 or 6 Africans in management positions in 1953. The number increased to 42 Ghanaians in 1961, corresponding to 33 percent of the staff, and by 1968 the percentage had risen to 67.

Could the firms have Africanised earlier? Only if there had better educational facilities on the Coast. Only in the mid-forties were training facilities being expanded. The firms, particularly Cadburys, beginning in the twenties and especially in the thirties, made scholarships available to Ghanaians, and encouraged the expansion of such educational facilities as Achimota College. In these respects the firms were innovative. Certainly some small portion of the profits from the concerns went into these efforts. The firms began to employ Africans in higher positions during the War. In light of the firm's standards for top positions in the thirties, we can say that they were probably now motivated by an enlighted self-interest.

By hindsight one can say that more should have been done. How much more would have been possible in education? Was this not an area for government initiative?

Some students of Ghanaian affairs speak of Africanisation as a second step to economic provisions in the development of the nation, but from our studies it is obvious that Africanisation occurred along with other factors which contributed to the establishment of a modern nation, including economic developments, governmental stability, and educational provisions.[48]

7

THE INDEPENDENCE ROUTE:
2. THE POLITY AND THE ECONOMY

Both the British government and the Coastal administration, during the last part of the forties, directed their efforts toward economic and political changes in the Gold Coast, supporting the move toward self-government and toward more Coastal economic activities. After World War II the first major thrust in these areas came from general policy directives issued by the Colonial Office in London. Just after the war the London office, because of the close communication between London and the Colonial Administration, was better equipped than ever to oversee and carry through policy development in the Colonies. But the London office had by that time begun to move toward political decentralization and self-government in the colonies.[1] Thus, by the late forties, political and economic policies had become local concerns, and decisions were made in the Gold Coast rather than in London.

Sir Alan Burns, as governor during World War II, was instrumental in providing for more political representation of Gold Coasters. Under Burns's administration the Legislative Council made constitutional provisions for some African representation. The Council in 1946 was made up of elected Africans, nominated Africans, and nominated Europeans. Some Europeans were nominated by the Chambers of Commerce and Mines, and therefore would be representative of expatriate businesses. Hailed as a grand step forward in 1946, these efforts were judged by the 1949 Committee on Constitutional Reform, most often referred to as the Coussey Commission, to have been inadequate. This commission, authorized by the Colonial Office, was the first to be composed entirely of Africans from the Gold Coast, and was formed as the direct result of criticisms made by the earlier Watson commission (see above Chapter 5). Both commissions found that the 1946 provisions for African participation were inadequate.[2]

Business representatives were able, through deputations and consultations, as well as Chamber of Commerce nominees, to express their views to members of the council and the government. Sir Alan noted that every colonial officer had a number of business people in various communities whom he could consult and whose advice he could trust.[3] Business seldom commented on or became involved in discussions about constitutional changes, except in regard to its own voice in the representative institutions, although most business representatives became watchful observers of political changes involving Ghanaian participation. The major part that the companies took in the independence movement in West Africa, according to Sir Alan, was to contribute to all "parties". It was normal course to contribute to all "parties", with the probable objective of gaining assistance later (see above pp. 63-68, 89). Sir Alan went on to note that the companies took no part in pressuring for or against independence.[4]

A major exception to this policy by business was the 1951 visit to the Coast by two British MP's, L. D. Gammans and Wing-Commander Cooper. It was thought that these men had been sponsored by the chairman of Ashanti Goldfields, Major-General Sir Edward Spears, who had been a member of the British Parliament earlier in his career. Spears, it was believed, wished to support the more conservative political factions rather than the faction urging immediate independence. A letter in the *Financial Times* from the General, however, denied the rumor of his support of Gammans and Cooper.[5] According to Spears, the MP's visited the Gold Coast at the invitation of the Chamber of Mines, and the invitation stated:

No obligation whatsoever is attached, and Members would be perfectly free to go anywhere and see anybody they wished. Our responsibility would merely extend to looking after them when they were visiting the mines, and transporting them from one to the other. There would be nothing to prevent our guests visiting Nigeria or any other part of the West Coast of Africa on their own responsibility. We are taking this step in the belief that we can only derive benefits from as many people as possible seeing our mines.[6]

The *West Africa* reports of this visit tend, nevertheless, to imply support from the Ashanti Goldfields.[7] In any event General Spears often personally approached MP's on topics of concern to him. On the question of self-government he did contact the Secretary of State for the Colonies, James Griffiths, probably because of the mine's concern about confiscation of property. Neither CAST nor Cadburys were known to have made personal contacts, but they may have had some representations.[8] Generally the British business firms indicated that their economic and future investment policies on the Coast would be determined by changes on the political front. In fact, all the concerns, after independence, significantly modified their activities on the Coast.

They continued with Coastal activities, but very quickly redeployed their resources to conform with governmental regulations and restrictions. For instance, controls over profits leaving the country brought significant redevelopment of Coastal activities during the sixties.

The Gold Coast Government and Business

The Coussey Commission's recommendations for constitutional changes were beginning to be implemented in 1950 and led in 1951 to Coastal self-government through the indigenous population vote for representatives.

At the time of the election Kwame Nkrumah, leader of the Convention People's Party, was in prison for his role in earlier disturbances but nevertheless stood for election in Accra Central. After the CPP's election success, the Governor, Arden-Clarke, ordered Nkrumah's release from prison to lead the government. During the fifties the opposition, which included the Togoland Congress (founded in 1951 by Ewes), the Northern People's Party (formed in 1954 in the Protectorate) and the National Liberation Movement (formed in 1954 by Ashantis), became known as the United Party. The 1958 Avoidance of Discrimination Act provided that parties should not be formed on ethnic bases. The two major issues of the decade were the realization of self government and independence and the creation of a unitary or federal state. Most of the opposition supported a federation.

British businesses were seldom directly involved in support of one side or the other on these issues. Involvements of the firms were mainly related to indigenous training and improvement of conditions related to business activities.

Political Training. Early in the thirties Cadburys had begun a program of active support for secondary education facilities, as demonstrated by its endowment of Achimota and its scholarship funds. These activities were noted in the Report on Africanisation in the Civil Service. After World War II, UAC also began to contribute to scholarship funds.[9] These efforts indirectly assisted in the training of Africans with sufficient education to become administrative personnel and later political leaders.

A 1952 memorandum from the manager of Holts Coast Administration Department reveals an enlightened self-interest motivation in the firm's willingness to support the political appointments of its African staff:

Under the elections for the Houses of Assembly and House of Representatives in the new Nigerian Constitution one of our African Produce Buyers has been elected a member for his constituency.

The question has arisen as to the company's attitude towards such political careerists and it has been decided that our policy is to encourage our African staff to such positions in their own country, more particularly where they may be old and trusted servants of the company. Although each individual case which may arise in the future will of course be considered on its merits, we think it is worthwhile stating a policy on these matters for the guidance of our General Managers.[10]

It was also recommended that the successful candidates be allowed a leave of absence and that "the difference between the salary they were enjoying with the company and the emoluments they may receive as a result of their political work by way of living expense" be made up by the company. The memo concluded that "not only will such members who have commercial knowledge and experience be of great value to the future development of Nigeria on the right lines but, if they are successful, they will also be of value to the company".[11] These recommendations clearly demonstrate the writer's awareness of the value of a firm's members being involved in politics, and the potential benefit to the firm.

Labor Organization. Efforts to establish labor organizations on the West Coast were strongly supported by Colonial policy in 1947, assisted by technical working parties from the Colonial Office in London. The Creech-Jones Papers reflect such policies, as do Creech-Jones' statements about development and labor organization in the colonies. He displayed an interest in colonial development and self-government as a member of parliament as early as the thirties. He asked pertinent questions of the government about African colonial policy. He was also a driving force in the Fabian Society's Colonial Bureau, which was responsible for publishing informative tracts on colonial affairs during the Second World War and was the first group in England to do so. Thus when Creech-Jones entered the Labour Cabinet as colonial secretary, he was well-versed in the problems of the colonies and had already developed some theoretical programs for bringing more independence to these areas. His own writings indicated his concern for cooperative developments, labor organizations, economic development programs, and efforts toward self-government in the colonies.[12]

The business firms trading on the Coast did not make statements about labor organizations, probably because the firms did not employ many workers who would have been involved in the early labor organizational efforts of the forties. Their workers were already members of house unions. As we have seen, they discussed at length training for clerical and managerial staffs.

After World War II labor laws were introduced as a result of Colonial Office policy and for the benefit of the returning soldiers. The major support of unionization on the Coast came from the Convention People's Party, which controlled the government after 1951. A centrally organized labor group did evolve by 1960 in Ghana through the Trades Union Congress and through the efforts of the Convention People's Party, but was never established in Nigeria.[13]

Mining. By 1951 the Gold Coast stood in sixth place among the world's gold-producing regions, with an annual production exceeding half a million ounces. The ore at Obuasi contains one ounce of gold to the ton, considered to be a very rich assay.[14] F. J. Erroll, Member of Parliament' and a director of the Ashanti Goldfields, explained, after a technical mission to Obuasi, that "for a Colony rapidly developing towards a high degree of self-government a stable and prosperous gold mining industry is one of the keys to success". He also gave examples of the cooperation between European and Africans:

Instead of a mere mining town, in which the mine owns all the houses and property, the Ashanti Corporation has been cooperating with the local Council. Obuasi is a town in its own right. The Company will build some houses, the Council many others. Services, such as water, sewage and electricity, are being worked out on a joint basis.[15]

In 1938 there had been three diamond companies in the Birim district, including CAST, which had a prosperous year, and the Holland Syndicate.[16] By 1950 diamond production was exceeding 1,000,000 carats in some years. The companies held mining leases through different arrangements. The customary land tenure lease, although differing from one district to another, conditioned the European holdings possible on the Coast. Mining rights were usually arranged on lease basis with chiefs, and European settlers were not encouraged, since European conceptions of ownership were not normally practiced on the Coast.[17]

In 1958 a Commission of enquiry into concessions heard testimony from the mine operators and other associated organizations, such as the chamber of mines, chiefs, and local administrations. The major concerns were the lease and tenure arrangements, smuggling and illicit mining, and the organization and operations of the companies.[18] The Chamber of Mines urged that the existing Concessions Ordinance be maintained, and that existing rules regarding termination of leases be retained.[19]

The Ghana Diamond Winners' Association urged that a cooperative marketing society be organized.[20] CAST submitted a lengthy report which discussed the organization of the company and such major problems as smuggling and illicit mining and security, and also the effect of CAST housing and educational programs on the area.[21] The training programs related mainly to mining activities and were described in the last chapter; they cost around £35,000 per year by 1962. CAST in that year employed around 2,700 workers. Approximately 70 percent were housed in rent-free quarters. According to a CAST report, an ambitious building program was continuing to extend the facilities and noted that

Already the villages have won a reputation for their cleanliness, and this coupled with the brightly painted houses, flowering shrubs and trees combines to make them an example to all who pass through the Company area. Filtered water is now supplied to most parts of the Camp and plans are afoot to extend electricity to the townships which, when completed, will compare favourably with any to be found elsewhere in Ghana.[22]

CAST indicated that large capital expenditures had been incurred in the past few years and that such expenditures could only be justified by the company "holding a Concession area of sufficient extent to supply adequate reserves to warrant the investment required". Finally, the memorandum concluded,

The best use of the country's diamond resources is made by large scale operations backed by continuous infusions of fresh capital and the best available technique for mineral recovery. In this way the landowners, by way of rents and royalties, and the Government, by way of duties and taxes, derive the maximum financial benefit from the mining of such resources.[23]

The White Paper report of the Commission made several recommendations regarding concessions which were supported by the government. In regard to future mineral grants, the Commission stated:

We are of the view that minerals (including oil and natural gases) should become vested in the Governor-General as representing the State, similarly as in the Northern Region, and administered as regards future grants by way of extension to the other Regions of Ghana of the existing Minerals Ordinance which applies to the Northern Region.[24]

The government accepted the Commission recommendation and proposed:

to carry out an urgent examination into the question of how timber and mineral rights can be vested in the State in such a way as to protect rights held under existing concessions. It is the intention of the Government to introduce legislation by which mineral rights shall become vested in the Government.[25]

The Commission went on to recommend that "the State should also participate in the equity share capital of the mining companies to the extent of 51 percent."[26] Such investments "should be made in a form and with the view to increase the yield deriving from the country's reserves as compared with present investments and with a view to assure effective influence by the Government on the business of the respective companies." The government's response was that it

does not therefore consider that mining companies should necessarily be singled out as the concerns in which the Government should invest, but should an occasion arise when for a particular economic or financial advantage it was desirable for the Government to acquire an interest in the equity of any new or existing mining company the Government would most certainly consider doing so.[29]

Agricultural Improvement. Even though the firms were not directly involved in food production and the production of cocoa, they did at times indicate through individual advice and company memoranda the need for increased food production and improved agricultural techniques. The concern was, of course, indirect but was related to the ability of the Gold Coaster to buy the firms' products or supply the cocoa needed by the manufacturers. A few examples of the firms' statements on agriculture will illustrate.

• In a post-World War II meeting about food shortages, Mr. FitzGerald, now Sir Patrick, indicated that it was not only the farmers who could assist with increased food production: "Mining and timber concerns and others should be encouraged to give their employees time off to cultivate plots or gets labour to cultivate their land for them with the object of growing enough food for their own needs. The schools could also do a lot about growing more food."[28] These suggestions are among the first urging diversification of agriculture. Cocoa, as we have noted, continued to occupy the major attention of the farmers. Even today systems of growing and distributing food stuffs are frequently inadequate and lead to situations in which governments are overthrown and the military takes over.

In earlier chapters we noted the concern of the firms, particularly Cadburys, for improvements in cocoa farming. Since the thirties Cadburys has advised governments about the quality of cocoa as well as improvement in farming techniques. Concern for quality is still an important focus of Cadburys.[29]

The Holts records note that just after the Second World War an additional presentation was made to the Colonial Secretary in London by one of the firms. Mr. R. I. Edwards of Holts raised questions about the profitability of such activities as maintaining the pig farm and manufacturing bacon after the troops had left the Coast, in view of the anticipated reduction in demand. The Department of Agriculture, according to the reply, did not intend to launch a large-scale enterprise, and hoped that the farm would soon be taken over by a cooperative society.[30]

Timber. Discussions about timber development also occurred and such development was supported by Unilever in the forties and UAC near the time of Ghanaian Independence. Professor Richardson, during his 1944 visit, observed the difficulties of transportation, and the physical toils involved in the timber and logging operations. In discussing solutions to the problems, he suggested that "Small scale capital would enable the Gold Coast to obtain tractors and other machinery which where necessary could be hired to operators".[31] A 1948 report on the Takoradi-Axim Forest District noted that the greater portion of timber exported was in log form. In addition, the average monthly amount of timber exported in 1948 from Takoradi-Axim district was around 11,780 tons, of which 64 percent was mahogany.[32] By 1955 timber had become a large enough export for the government to consider reasonable control. The Commission of Enquiry into Concessions recommended that a state-owned Timber Marketing Board be established. The government, however, accepted the recommendation only in principle, "but in so doing the government will safeguard the property and future prospects of investors in the industry".[33] It proposed to set up a Timber Marketing Board which would, at first, deal only with one type of timber, the wawa. By this time UAC was redeploying its resources on the Coast and by 1947 were supporting timber operations, including a small mill.[34]

Primary Industry. To complete the economic picture of the Coast and the role of the British firms in its development, mention should be made of efforts to establish primary industrial activities. The Development Act was first passed in 1929 under Sydney Webb. By 1945 the Colonial Development and Welfare Act was in full operation under Oliver Stanley. The government was asked to prepare plans to improve education and social and economic conditions.[35] No major discussions of industrial development occurred in the forties. The highlights of development on the Coast during this decade were in political structure and constitutional reforms.

As indicated earlier, the British firms under review seldom advised the Colonial Office or the government about economic activities that were outside their immediate scope of operations. The social conscience of business enterprises on the Coast and elsewhere in the world and thus the crusades for new developments was not to develop until the 1970's. British commercial concerns thus were to play little or no part in efforts to establish power sources, such as the Volta River scheme, despite the comments of the Colonial Secretary in 1943:

1. Private enterprise must have a place in post-war Colonial development;
2. It is intended to form an Economic Advisory Board or Committee in Whitehall;
3. I believe that after the war there will be found to be industrialists with a real desire, apart from the profit motive, to assist in the task of imperial development . . . well, miracles do happen . . ."[36]

The Colonial Secretary, in an interview with the West Africa Merchants, stated that he had been misrepresented by Hansard and that instead of saying "Miracles do happen," he had replied: "I do not believe in miracles, which is why I have never tried to form any other party than a Conservative Party."[37] Despite these words, there is no indication that an economic advisory committee was established after the war.

Colonial Service personnel going to the Gold Coast just after World War II were instructed to assist toward independence, but no one thought that independence would come in the next decade.[38] The Volta River power development scheme did, however, occupy attention in this period. The first studies were made under the Colonial Office and the administration during the war period. The firms on the Coast—merchant and manufacturers—took very little part, as noted above, in the planning 'for this major development, though on occasion during the twenty-year planning period agents of the firms mentioned the project.[39]

The Colonial Development Corporation was also operating in the forties, but no plans were sponsored under this program in the Gold Coast. The Act provided for the Colonial Administration to submit project plans to the Colonial Office; the financial arrangements were then to be jointly sponsored by the local government and Great Britain. The chairman of the Corporation came to the Coast while Governor Creasy was in office, but no arrangements for development were made under the Act.[40] (See above, pp. 8-9.)

Secondary Industry—Business and Markets. Cadburys and UAC have contributed to the development of the Ghanaian economy through technical assistance on special problems, such as marketing cocoa and establishing local control over distribution of goods; schemes for marketing cocoa and the distribution arrangements have been reviewed in earlier chapters. George Cole, in his testimony for UAC to the Commission on the Disturbances in 1948, noted:

The Company has always regarded the introduction of industries merely for the sake of industrialisation as being politically and economically wrong. It desires to see the establishment of an industry in any field in which such an industry would be economically sound, and would be able, either to export its products under competitive conditions with the remainder of the world, or to market them locally without putting up the price unduly. The Company has regarded it as fundamental to any industry that it should create wealth within the Colony. It does not regard processing locally of imported raw materials as being necessarily sound economy unless the product can be marketed at a lower price than if imported in a manufactured state.[41]

It was also noted that the development of any plantations on a European scale in the Gold Coast was precluded by political policy and by the opposition of the people to the alienation of land. There were some raw materials in the country, such as timber and aluminum, which, the report noted, could be developed. (The UAC, as mentioned earlier, had a subsidiary operation in 1948 involved in logging, saw-milling, and later plywood and board manufacturing, called the African Timber and Plywood Ltd.).[42] The UAC memorandum continued by noting that the company had taken the view that "it is not its business to intrude in the cottage or peasant industries, but only to give them all the encouragement it can". For this reason the company regarded "the cottage weaving industry and the manufacture of pottery, and tile-making and furniture-making and kindred industries as affairs properly left to the Africans themselves".[43] When European skill and supervision were required, the company had undertaken such projects as a "refrigerating business, mineral water manufacture, and bacon-making". In addition the company had put its distributing organization "at the disposal of many other concerns producing their own commodities in the Gold Coast". With other firms it distributed "beer for the Accra Brewery, packed petroleum products for the oil companies, salt from the producers in Addah Keta district," and made some arrangements for distribution of a small quantity of cloth from Togoland.[44]

Arthur Creech-Jones wrote Mr. Mellor of UAC about the firm's reputation on the Coast, based on observations made while he visited there in 1947.[45] He first noted five areas of annoyance to the African:

(a) too little of the profit secured on the products of his countries comes back into Africa;

(b) alien interests exploit the natural resources and minerals and leave little of their value for the social and economic development of the people;

(c) the prices of primary producers are too low and where wage labour is employed there is too little welfare and the wage standards are poor;

(d) the activities of brokers and agents discourage African enterprises; and

(e) a fatalism coupled with a deterioration in crafts and small industries is creeping over the scene because of the economic power influence and strongly entrenched interests of the big concerns.[46]

Creech-Jones went to say[47] that Mr. Mellor had "long and intimate experience in West Africa" and he therefore did not pretend to have answers for all the problems but only grouped in seven areas suggestions that seemed immediately applicable.[48] These seven areas included cooperative enterprises, prices on primary products, control of brokers, returning royalties on minerals to West Africa for economic and social development, use of resources for social welfare of the West Africans, establishment of scholarships (above, Chapter 6), and the representation of big business on developmental boards and other Governmental agencies:

(a) UAC should make it known that it will encourage cooperative enterprise of all kinds in Africa and deal with the co-operatives . . . that it will encourage African enterprise in small industries . . . and that it will assist in achieving higher standards of efficiency in some of the native products by supporting collectivist experiments.

(b) UAC will try to secure a reasonable but fair price for primary products, use its influence in the regulation of prices to this end, encourage in world commodity schemes recognition of the rights of labour, its fair reward and proper welfare provision. . . .

(c) UAC will urge its Agents to be considerate of African enterprise . . . and will see that the Brokers are effectively controlled to this end.

(d) UAC will return all future royalties on minerals for the economic and

social development of the countries of West Africa; where royalties are drawn it will direct its influence on companies and government that good conditions of employment shall operate. . . .

e) Big Business ought to show a greater philanthropy in the country which gives it its profits and products. . . . Schoolls (sic), Research Stations, Libraries, Reading Rooms, Recreation places, Clinics, Hospitals, Meeting places, and the thousand and one social institutions and amenities which add something to living or help to improve it or give us more scientific knowledge to manage it—I saw no evidence—only a drain of values and wealth away from the country. . . .

(f) Scholarships to this country, technical institutes, wings to university institutions, more science laboratories, teacher training colleges, and many other things may be matters for the Colonial Government, but both the people and the Colonial Governments with the existing limited resources, make financial provision near to impossible. Yet much wealth goes overseas and there seems a conspiracy to compel the colonial people to live on the lowest possible margins. Big business could help.

(g) Big Business is represented on Development Boards in the Legislative Councils, on Governors Executives, on Municipalities and so on. Its representatives could take a lead for ordered progress, improved social services, development works, improved agriculture, more balanced economies.[49]

Creech-Jones again reiterated the desirability of government involving expatriate business in planning for development of the various colonies. A similar statement had been made in 1943 by the previous Secretary of State for the Colonies. If we examine the planning for development thereafter, we find, however, that businesses were involved only in the affairs immediately related to their operations. There were business representatives in the Coast on the Legislative Council through the Chamber of Commerce's representatives, but no major effort was made to plan with business for specific new developments in the economy.

Business Contribution to Development, 1940-1956

Although the removal of profits from the Coast by the expatriate firms during this period constitutes exploitation, the firms, by reinvesting profits on the Coast, contributed to its development, and in this respect we may characterize them as innovative. During this period UAC continued to diversify its Coastal activities in merchandise trade, to serve as an agent in buying cocoa for the Cocoa Marketing Board, and to expand its operations in timber and other areas. Cadburys also took profits out of the Gold Coast, especially by continuing to process their cocoa overseas. On the other hand, Cadburys continued their support for cocoa research and for education and community centre schemes. Holts began to limit its operations on the Coast but did reinvest in the Coastal motor industry.

The firms' support of economic development on the Coast during this pre-independent period thus fostered continuation of a market for the buying and selling of goods and produce, employment of labor, and, indirectly, training of personnel for economic and later political pursuits. Only on a few occasions did any of the firms directly enter the political arena by supporting a political faction. But their concerns were usually represented adequately by persons selected to serve on boards and by personnel 'involved in representation functions.

8

POST–INDEPENDENCE:
DEVELOPMENT POLICIES

After independence, members of British business served spasmodically as consultants on development programs. The local manager of Elder Dempster Ltd. served on the Agricultural Development Corporation Board, and W. R. Feaver served on the Industrial Development Corporation Board for a three-year period from 1957 to 1961.[1] Firms remaining in Ghana continued to bring matters of specific concern to the attention of governmental officials and, from time to time, to Nkrumah or, later, to appropriate committees of the National Liberation Council. In the development of various programs, the National Redemption Council consulted business personnel and firms.[2]

Cocoa Marketing
P. T. Bauer has questioned the policy of the Marketing Board in the fifties and its function as described in the 1947 statute.[3] The statute provided that the Board was to promote the interest of the producers by means of price stabilization.[4] Bauer contended that by the fifties the board was becoming an instrument for socialization of savings.[5] Income was being withheld from the farmer for the reserve funds and used for loans to the government. The policy became more evident with independence, and in the 1960-61 season the Board made loans to the Ghana government amounting to £G 26.3 million. Killick points out that if the Board's policies did in fact discourage expansion of cocoa production, as Bauer also maintained, "they may well have been, albeit unwittingly, all to the good in view of the development of the world market conditions in the '50's".[6]

Soon after independence, the Ghanaian government reviewed the Cocoa Marketing Board activities. The government decided to take over from the foreign firms the purchase of cocoa from the Ghanaian farmer, and then consulted with the firms about the best means of making the change at very short notice. By 1961 the government had also decided to withdraw to Accra the London Office of the Cocoa

Table 7.   FINANCIAL STATEMENT 1956-61 COCOA MARKETING BOARD 1957-1961 (*Ghana £*)

	1956/57	*1957/58*	*1958/59*	*1959/60*	*1960/61*
Local loans to government less Repayments	12,535,594	11,730,067	22,503,224	26,926,431	26,282,192
Net operating surplus/loss	5,193,838	6,539,062	8,541,809	4,215,015	——
Cocoa rehabilitation reserve	2,500,000	3,500,000	4,500,000	3,323,726	——
General trading reserve	6,106,925	427,600	——	——	——
General reserve	2,500,000				
Local development grant reserve	410,00	773,000	500,000	——	——
Endowment and Capital grant (University College of Ghana)					
Expenditure on swollen roots	70,000	640	200,000	——	——
Annual grant to United Ghana Farmers' Council	——	300,000	197,827	——	——
Produce inspection	——	210,000	100,000	——	——

Source: Ghana Cocoa Marketing Board, 14th Annual Report and Accounts, September 30, 1961.

Marketing Company, which was selling cocoa on the world market. Thus in 1961 the Cocoa Marketing Board had the sole right to export and buy for export. The United Ghana Farmers' Council Co-operatives were the Board's sole agents for purchasing cocoa and were responsible for storage and transportation to the port. The Ministry of Agriculture Produce Inspection Division was responsible for inspection and grading.[7] The financial status[8] of the Board during the early sixties is reflected in Tables 7 and 8.[9]

The Ghanaian government requested Cadburys to allow Mr. Feaver and two experienced cocoa buyers to serve as an advisory team during the transitional period. This team served from 1961 to 1963. It gave advice as the system went from many licensed buying agents to the single buyer—the United Cocoa Farmers' Council.[10]

Table 8. PURCHASES GHANA COCOA MARKETING BOARD
(Long Tons)

Year	Main	Mid	Total
1947/48	203,808	3,751	207,559
1948/49	269,051	9,321	278,372
1949/50	246,443	1,391	247,834
1950/51	258,282	3,941	262,223
1951/52	206,904	3,759	210,663
1952/53	243,385	3,597	246,982
1953/54	205,793	4,900	210,693
1954/55	206,445	13,662	220,107
1955/56	218,020	10,772	228,792
1956/57	261,094	2,619	263,713
1957/58	194,623	11,882	206,505
1958/59	225,860	29,628	225,488
1959/60	291,529	25,411	316,940
1960/61	420,647	11,596	432,243
1961/62	397,133	12,278	409,411
1962/63	381,947	39,789	421,736
1963/64	370,685	50,360	421,045
1964/65	556,642	15,080	571,722
1965/66	396,143	4,057	400,200
Total	5,554,434	257,794	5,812,228

Source: Ghana Cocoa Marketing Board, typescript, July 1966.

When the National Liberation Council was established in 1966 and questions arose about the reorganization of cocoa marketing, the British firms showed no desire to become buying agents in Ghana again.[11] Soon afterward a Committee of Enquiry on Local

Purchasing of Cocoa was convened and chaired by J. C. de Graft Johnson. The Committee in its deliberations made use of the recommendations of the Cadbury and business representatives' advisory team. It reported on July 23, 1966. Among a number of suggestions about the details of coca buying, it recommended that more producer representatives be put on the Board, that the Ghana Co-op Marketing Association be granted a license and return to the buying field, and that the Ghana Cocoa Buying Organisation be established, but not as a civil service department. The committee also suggested that certain aspects of cocoa purchasing and job evaluation be undertaken, including the establishment of an advisory and inspectorate committee to report to the NLC.[12] This 1966 commission also recommended the establishment of a tax committee to give advice about the implementing the report, as had the Cadbury team in 1961.

The farmers, during this period, were concerned about the local price of cocoa. By September 1966 the price to the farmer was revised upward but not significantly. By 1970 purchases of cocoa were reported to be higher than in the previous season. According to a January 1970 issue of *West Africa,* the purchases after nineteen weeks totaled 327,835 tons compared with 296,015 tons in the same season of 1961.[13] (See Table 9.)

The United Ghana Farmers Council ceased to be sole buyer of cocoa after the coup. This council was dissolved and its functions were transferred to the Purchasing Department of the Cocoa Marketing Board. Its staff also was transferred and received increases in salaries. With these increases and lower cocoa purchases, a 3.8 million cedis loss was expected in 1967. In 1966 the Board received a 21.5 million cedis loss on cocoa tradings as compared to a 29.5 million cedis loss in 1965.[14]

The declining price of cocoa had by 1972 twice coincided with a military coup in Ghana. These prices combined with inflation and shortages of goods at home were mentioned after both coups as major factors contributing to unrest and discontent among the people. Accompanying these problems were criticisms of both governments' handling of the continued pressure from international creditors, and accusations of corruption and/or extravagant standards of living among governemental officials. Busia did not have the resources, however, nor was he in office long enough to have opportunities to develop the economic or prestige-building programs that were the butt of so much anti-Nkrumah sentiment in 1966. Among reasons for the resentment against Busia were his efforts to curtail personal spending and extravagant living practices among government officials, and for introducing taxes and controls in efforts to improve the international standing of Ghana's balance of payments.[15] In the background, cocoa prices, still not controlled

Table 9. GHANA: INTERNAL ALLOCATION OF F.O.B. COCOA BEAN PRICE FOR THE PERIOD 1959/60—1971/72

	1959/60	1960/61	1961/62	1962/63	1963/64	Oct. 1964 Feb. 1965	Mar.- Dec. 1965	1966	1967	1968	1969	1970	1970/71	1971/72 (est.)
						(New Cedis per long ton)								
Price paid to producer	224.30	224.00	224.00	224.00	224.00	224.00	214.68	153.44	186.66	245.75	270.10	298.62	298.67	300.00
Farmers contribution 2nd Development Plan	44.39	44.80	44.80	44.80	—	—	—	—	—	—	—	—	—	—
Allowance payable to buying agents	22.58	21.95	21.11	24.88	28.48	28.48	15.84	25.08	26.28	33.76	37.05	38.65	38.66	40.45
Storage time allowance	-.22	-.31	-.03	-.15	-.16	-.15	-.28	-.06	-.02	-.20	-.24	-.23	-.34	-.25
Export and local duty	125.09	75.62	58.68	63.85	78.64	66.15	32.33	49.23	111.04	227.81	380.50	486.02	317.33	320.00
Railway and road transport	10.03	9.65	10.58	10.77	10.81	9.54	11.32	11.25	12.75	12.40	14.41	12.44	15.96	13.92
Lighterage, other shipping charges, etc.	2.61	2.97	2.82	2.91	3.03	2.80	4.93	2.75	3.17	2.78	3.74	2.97	4.42	3.05
Fumigation expenses	-.68	-.49	-.28	-.34	-.52	-.67	-.40	-.64	-.75	1.08	1.23	-.91	1.24	-.59
Finance & bank charges	1.14	6.29	5.56	6.64	6.68	13.22	7.88	11.06	4.63	8.70	8.80	2.67	6.73	13.50
Administration (salaries), office exps., board meetings, etc. portion of cost of bags borne by board	6.48	3.98	6.10	3.71	2.56	24.46	3.82	2.32	2.66	5.24	4.81	5.10	8.68	8.75
Amounts written off	8.03	—	—	—	—	—	—	—	—	—	—	—	—	—
Total f.o.b. price cocoa beans	437.52	398.09	373.96	382.05	354.83	369.47	291.49	255.83	347.96	537.72	720.88	847.61	692.03	700.51

Source: Ghana Cocoa Marketing Board, Accra. UN Conference on Trade and Development, Marketing and Distribution of Cocoa, February 6, 1973. TD/B/C.1/132.

through international agreement, perhaps remain most responsible for the unrest leading to the military overthrow of unpopular governments. The NLC and Dr. Busia's government devoted much attention to rectifying the grave international economic situation that Ghana faced in the sixties, and continued efforts toward further economic development within the country.

Ghana's export earnings after independence failed to grow at the same rate as imports. By the mid-sixties a large deficit existed in the balance of trade, and in 1965-66 the price of cocoa dropped dramatically, leaving Ghana in a crisis. After the first coup the NLC and then Dr. Busia rescheduled the debt service charges through agreements in 1966, 1968 and 1970. In 1968, as preparations for a new constitutional government were under way the international price on cocoa rose, and with adjustment of the debt charges a surplus of export earnings reappeared, leaving a more healthy economic situation for the 1969 constitutional government. (International Monetary or World Bank funds were used after 1969 to control swollen shoot disease.) The rise was maintained only briefly, however, as the market price for cocoa continued to fluctuate. By December 1971 Dr. Busia had announced a 40 percent devaluation of the cedi and was having difficulties meeting both international debt commitments and internal demands for lower prices and better supplies of goods.

On January 13, 1972, a second coup, led by Colonel I. K. Acheampong, took over the government in Accra while Dr. Busia was in London. The constitutional government was charged with the devaluation of the cedi and restrictions on gasoline for officers, as well as other restrictions on general living standards for government and military officers. Colonel Acheampong announced the formation of a National Redemption Council and of a committee of civilians and government officials to review the present arrangements for purchasing cocoa. In February 1975 the Board became administratively responsible to the new Ministry of Cocoa Affairs.

Other Economic Developments

Although cocoa continues to account for around 50 percent of Ghana's exports each year (55 percent in 1969, with 370,000 tons worth 219.7 million cedis, and in 1970), the independence government emphasized until the 1972 coup the development of secondary and primary industries.[16] By the time of independence, more rapidly during the sixties, the merchandise firms were changing from suppliers of cloth and food products to suppliers of motors and equipment. In addition, UAC and Unilever worked with the government after independence to redeploy their investments. Such redeployment included a department store in 1956, a vehicle assembly for Bedford trucks to the government in 1958, a veneer and plywood factory in 1959, a Kumasi brewery in 1960, and a soap factory in 1963. In February 1966, when the coup occurred, Unilever considered giving assistance to the government in its efforts to make operative a wax block factory which had been built by a so-called turn-key concern. The directors of the British concerns were able until 1966 to approach the president when political and administrative problems arose.[17] Holts had moved out of Ghana soon after independence, except for the motors industry, which was still operating in 1966.[18]

Timber came close to cocoa in value as an export in 1969. Its value was 39.1 millions cedis. In that year timber represented a higher percentage of exports than gold. It was now being handled by a Timber Marketing Board, but its development was hindered by transportation problems.[19].

In the mining industry the Ashanti Goldfields has been on the Coast for the longest period. CAST was there in early twentieth century, mining diamonds. Both concerns have continued to operate in Ghana; as predicted in the Concessions Enquiry, however, the government did take over five mines in 1961 and began to control the dividends that the companies could take out of Ghana.[20] Ashanti Goldfields obtained a new 50-year lease beginning January 1, 1969, even though the old lease did not expire until 1986. The company was taken over by Lonrho, which promised to increase the milling capacity of the mine from 45,000 tons to 80,000 tons, and to issue to the government 20 percent of Ashanti's shares. If the dividends on the shares fall short of the royalties under the old lease, Lonrho has agreed to compensate the government. General Spears, former chairman of Ashanti Goldfields, joined the board of Lonrho.[21]

The government also began to enter the fields of banking and shipping. Before independence the dominant banks were the Bank of West Africa and Barclays DCO. Although these banks still operate in Ghana, there are also the newly established Ghana Commercial Bank and the Bank of Ghana (Central Bank). In shipping, the government set up the Black Star Shipping Line soon after independence. By 1964 it controlled a fleet of twelve ships. One of the first announcements of the National Redemption Council in January 1972 was of its intention to add "National" to the name: The Black Star Line (the National Shipping line of Ghana).[22]

In rural development the Nkrumah government attempted several agricultural improvement schemes, including mechanization and diversification of crops. The Busia government immediately concentrated on diversification by promoting the growth of rice and maize.[23]

Brief mention has already been made of the first independence government's efforts to control and at the same time attract primary and secondary industry. The Busia government immediately attempted to attract foreign business with reductions of some controls, particularly in sectors requiring high capital investment. In addition, local business promotion became the central focus of a parliamentary act of August 1970. A two-year development program was introduced by the National Liberation Council in 1967 and was continued on an annual basis by the 1969 government. The first annual plan emphasized increased economic growth rates from 3.5 to 5 percent, with industrial production from 10 to 15 percent. Among the development programs was an expansion program for the Akosombo Hydroelectric Power State under the Volta River Authority. In the areas of agricultural and industrial development, the National Redemption Council planned to appoint immediately civilian committees—composed of bankers, private businessmen, government officials, and economists—to review arrangements for the purchase of cocoa and the devaluation of the cedi (which was devalued by 40 percent in December 1971).[24] (See Table 10).

Table 10.   U.S. DOLLARS PER GHANA POUND/NEW CEDI:
1960-74

1960	2.80	1967	0.98[a,b]
1961	2.80	1968	0.98
1962	2.80	1969	0.98
1963	2.80	1970	0.98
1964	2.80[b]	1971	0.55[a]
1965	1.17	1972	0.78
1966	1.17[b]	1973	0.87
		1974	0.87

[a] Dates of change: July 8, 1967; December 27, 1971; and February 1972.
[b] On February 23, 1967, a new monetary unit, New Cedi, replaced Cedi at the rate of 1.2 Old Cedi per New Cedi.
Source: *Statistical Year Book*, 1972, 24th edition (UN Department of Economics and Social Affairs (New York, 1973). *International Financial Statistics*, 27, No. 4 (International Monetary Fund, Washington, D.C., 1974).

After the National Liberation Council was formed in 1966, business seemed to be acquiring a new role in government affairs. Some directors of the British firms in Ghana were consulted about various phases of economic policy. A Ghanaian who had been a civil servant in the Gold Coast administration and then in the independence administration until 1962 returned to Ghana in 1966 as a director of CAST. This director, Richard Quashie, not only served on the Economic Committee of the NLC but became minister of trade and industry in the Busia government. The National Redemption Council, through Acheampong, announced the intention of including businessmen on the committees which are to investigate the pressing economic problems of the country. A five-year plan for developing an independent economy based on resource potentials in Ghana and providing for fairer distribution was announced in January 1975.[25]

Toward New Internal and External Marketing Arrangements

Extreme examples of the breakdown of political institutions in Ghana, which probably resulted from the failures to initiate an international agreement on cocoa, are observed in the 1966 and 1972 military takeovers of the civil governements. Such new nations as Ghana, dependent on international markets, cannot develop political institutions with any stability until their economic problems are brought under control through rational systems of internal and international marketing, and through assistance from private and public sources for further development. Until such controls of the markets are realized, the political institutions will remain unstable and will be likely to fail with each new international economic clump in cocoa prices. As each economic crisis diminishes, new but temporary political arrangements can be expected to arise. The rise and fall of the Nkrumah and Busia governments, as well as the earlier disturbances on the Coast, are cases in point.[26]

Internal marketing of cocoa has been variously controlled by the statutory marketing board since 1947. Several changes in the structure were thought to bring the farmer closer to the board's operations, but as yet these measures have not been completely successful.[27] There is still need for the further involvement of farmers in the Board's activities, and for a more effective system of buying from the farmer. The New Zealand marketing board schemes, particularly for dairy products, could serve as effective models for both internal and external arrangements. They do allow for farmers' participation in agricultural policymaking and for an efficient system of buying from the farmer; processing of the product, however, is part of the system in New Zealand. In addition, New Zealand has a well established system for national politics.[28]

One essential feature for international stability involves the establishment of an international commodity agreement for cocoa. The British representatives to international cocoa conferences during the sixties and seventies usually came from the manufacturing and buying concerns. John Cadbury and W. R. Feaver, both of Cadburys, have both attended working sessions and conferences. Mr. Byles of Gill and Duffus—the firm responsible for setting an unofficial estimate for the London spot Ghana price of cocoa for the world market—has also participated in the discussions. As indicated above, in the April 1972 conference the manufacturers continued to insist on a low ceiling for the maximum price before quotas could be suspended and before the international machinery to use buffer stocks could go into operation.

An agreement was signed by enough producer and manufacturer nations to put the International Cocoa Authority into operation by mid 1973.[29] The price of cocoa has since been so strong that the authority has not needed to operate. The Cocoa Marketing Board released over 1 million cedis from the 1972-73 main crop sales for distribution through seven agencies to the cocoa farmers as bonuses.[30] During the 1975-76 season it was thought that the price was going to decline, yet at the beginning of the season the price was still strong. The United States, in the early seventies, did not sign the Cocoa Agreement or any other commodity agreement. By May 1975, however, the United States Secretary of State announced a unique policy of support for singular commodity agreements— each to be evaluated on its own merit.[31]

Certainly all the manufacturing nations should sign the agreement: in their own interest to maintain supply and in an enlightened interest to create a rational international market, so that the developing nations can realize economic stability. The Cocoa Agreement provides such a mechanism. Such economic stability depends first on the nation achieving a rational internal marketing mechanism. But ultimately the international market must be controlled though the efforts of the International Cocoa Authority.

9

THE CONTRIBUTION OF
EXPATRIATE FIRMS

The focus of this volume has been on the relation of British business to Gold Coast developments during the 1938-57 period. The key questions:

1. What were the innovative and exploitative aspects of the firms' influence on and contributions to economic development?
2. What was the role of business in policy-making and what was its relation to the Colonial Office?
3. Did the firms have the capacity to accelerate their contributions? Should they have been responsible for initiations of such developmental policies as education?
4. What was the role of the farmer in marketing board decisions? Did the farmer have an adequate understanding of the international market?

The conclusions that follow are based on materials cited in previous chapters, and gathered from Colonial Office records and reports, from Gold Coast government Archives, from the firms' records, and from interviews and private papers of former colonial and governmental officials, firms' personnel, and Ghanaians involved in the various events.

Business and Economic Development
British overseas businesses have been described both as neocolonialists and exploiters of the people, and as exporters of Western civilization, making possible modernization and urbanization of colonial areas. Both of these characterizations have simplified a rather complex situation, and have thereby confused the student of West African History. It would be more accurate to say that the firms were motivated to earn a profit through their activities on the Coast, but they also realized that this activity would be enhanced by increasing the buying power of the people. It is an

exaggeration to describe the firms as economic innovators, but by bringing trade, new goods, and industry to the Gold Coast, they fostered the change from a rural orientation to an exchange market and an urban economy.

Profits, Investment, Exploitation, Innovation. The firms' efforts were primarily directed toward realization of profits from the sale of cocoa on the world market and from the selling of goods on the Coast. Yet profits were limited in 1937 by a decline in world price and restricted from 1939 to 1946 by wartime controls. When controls were ended and enough supplies became available, the profits made continuation of trade possible and covered the cost of supplying the Coast. From the creation of the Cocoa Marketing Board until 1961, the firms acted only as buying agents for the Board. In the fifties and sixties the merchant firms invested more extensively as prescribed by the government, in other activities on the Coast.

It is true that, as distributors and manufacturers of goods elsewhere in the world, business has taken capital out of West Africa. Because of the agricultural basis of the West African economies, the West Africans received payment for raw materials or goods but did not retain within their own borders further profits from the processing and distribution of the goods. This condition is common to newly developing countries while they await capital investment. The United States, in 1880's was dependent of British capital; Canada in the 1970's is dependent on United States capital, and West Africa, still attempting to attract capital investments, is very much dependent on foreign capital. But foreign investment in cocoa has contributed to the development of a central monetary market in West Africa and has brought about conditions and motivation necessary for economic and national development.

Very few countries with small populations have been able to maintain their economies on the basis of agricultural exports, and at the same time to support economic development and modernization. One exception is New Zealand, which has thus far successfully avoided recurrent crises but only because it has enjoyed internal political stability. Since 1840 it has developed a homogeneous population which soon evolved a society which is both European and urban in character. (The Maori constitutes about five percent of the population. There has been steady integration between the Maori and European populations, more noticeably since the 1940's.) Ghana, on the other hand, with a large population, with differences in social traditions and without a European urban reference, has not yet stabilized its economic and political processes to the extent that the nation can weather the vicissitudes of the international cocoa market. Not until 1973 were producers and most manufacturers able to agree on conditions to control the market, as had earlier the coffee and tea interests. The international firms that manufacture cocoa still enjoy profits from the business, but the producers located in Ghana receive only the profits on agricultural production.

Exploitation of the economy was not, however, the sole result of the manufacturing and merchant firms' activities in this twenty-year period, 1937-57. There were too many governmental controls as well as informal controls to allow such a situation to occur. The firms themselves realized the advantages of continuing the market on the Coast by meeting the demands for goods which in effect gave them a market. During this period each firm contributed variously to the economic development of the Gold Coast.

One can accurately conclude that the investment of British business brought both favourable and unfavourable results. There were *innovative* characteristics—the investment of money increased demand for goods, and led ultimately to the demand by indigenous peoples for changes in the economic and social styles of their lives. Investments by business increased motivation for monetary exchanges and provided the basis for transition to urban and modern economics. But there were also *exploitive* characteristics—some resources were drained from the country, perhaps slowing development. Only if the West African nations form a viable, self sufficient regional economic unit can they build, as have the United States, Russia, China, and Europe, a system that is less dependent upon the rest of the world. Such regional unions, with an economic motivation, can develop further controls over common concerns.

The particular involvement of Cadburys, Holts, and UAC in capitalistic, exploitative, and innovative aspects of development is reviewed in Table 11. It covers four periods: the Cocoa Hold-Up, 1937-38; the war period, 1940-46; the period of developing self-government, 1947-57; and independence from 1957 to 1970. The firms could be criticized for not developing local manufacturing opportunities earlier; yet such enterprises, to be successful, must go hand in hand with local training and educational facilities.

Business and the Colonial Office:
Contributions to Developmental Policy

Generally, then, each impact of British business in West Africa from 1937 to 1957 has been a complex of favorable and unfavorable contributions to the local environment. Individually, the firms' contributions to economic and political development have varied during this period. The experience of Cadburys, UAC, and Holts demonstrates that specific British businesses exerted an influence on development policy in the Gold Coast and Ghana mainly when the firms initiated contacts first with the Colonial Office and then after 1948 with the Government. A review of the firms' records indicates that efforts to make contacts usually occurred at times of economic

Table 11.   DEGREE OF INVOLVEMENT BY CADBURYS, HOLTS, AND UAC. 1937-1970

Various Aspects[a] *(Illustrative)*	*1937-38*	*1940-46*	*1947-48 to 1957*	*1957-70*
CAPITALIST FEATURES				
Profits[b] motivation	UAC announces losses on cocoa. Firms attempted agreement to establish cocoa quotas for each firm.	Government control of buying and selling	UAC reduced profit on merchandise (1948)	Redeployment of resources in accord with government policy
Competition with African business	(See above)	A and B firms for cocoa and shipping allocations		
EXPLOITATION				
Overseas manufacturing	Chocolate continues to be manufactured overseas	Cadburys		Some local manufacturing
Overseas processing		Some local processing		Increase in local processing
INNOVATION				
Reinvestment within country		UAC timber	Holts motors	UAC plywood, soap (technical operations)
Policy initiation	Cadburys on quality of cocoa since 1930's	Government control, 1940		
Marketing	Agreement attempted on quotas for each firm.			

Marketing boards		Board (local) 1947 firms' agents of board	Board (producers)
New concerns, e.g. trading corporation. Training and scholarships Market economy	UAC late 1940's Cadburys began support of secondary schools in 1920's	Holts' management training, 1950's	GNTC Mining

All firms contributed to its realisation.

[a] Please refer above to p. 2, for definitions used.
[b] Detailed information about specific profits were not available. Access was available only to such published details as the UAC illustrations. For market prices of cocoa, see above, pp. 16-17, 55, 109, 134.

crises. Conclusions in this section are all based on documentary evidence: Colonial Office and governmental reports, records of business firms, and interviews with colonial and governmental officials. firms' personnel and Ghanaians variously involved—cited in the previous chapters.

Business: Initiator of Governmental Contacts. The 1937 cocoa crisis presented a unique example of contacts between business and the Colonial Office. Our review began in 1937 when the firms, through UAC initiative, formulated an Agreement to assist in the control of cocoa-trading conditions. The firms, in this period, first informed the Colonial Office in London of the Agreement, which then was to disperse the information to the government in Accra and supposedly to the farmers. The Cocoa Hold-Up resulted in large part from the governor's decision to hold this information until his questions about the advisability of the Agreement reached London. During the period when the firms' representatives were in Accra attempting to find a solution to the problems of the Hold-Up, there were further evidences of disagreement between the representatives in Accra, the London firms' representatives, and the Colonial Office, a disagreement due mainly to their various perspectives on the situation. The colonial administration's distrust of the firms represented a typical governmental reaction to business in the colonies before World War II. The second major result of the Hold-Up not fully realized by either the firms or the government in 1938, was the evidence that farmers could organize and offer a strong voice in the economic and political arena.

Another initiative from business arose through suggestions from Cadburys for World War II controls on cocoa marketing.

Business in Government and as Consultants. The war period produced unusual cooperation between business and government, as well as daily contact. A close partnership was evident between business firms handling cocoa and government departments both in London and in Accra. Following the suggestion of a Cadburys' representative, the Colonial Office did implement the scheme for controls and licensing for the buying of certain products, including cocoa. Personnel for the wartime operations were drawn from the manufacturing and business concerns as well as from the civil service, and the Joint West African Committee both on the Coast and in England served in a liaison capacity for these control operations. With the ending of war activities, some concerns and some British business federations questioned the advisability of these controls. When controls were withdrawn and wartime activities ceased, the close working relationship between business and the government, both in London and in the Coast, began to dissolve.

At the close of the war discussion about cocoa marketing boards in West Africa occupied the attention of the government, the Colonial Office, and the interested firms. The major questions about such schemes had been raised by the British firms in 1944 in discussions with the Colonial Office, resulting from a statement issued by the Secretary of State. During 1947 the boards were established by action of the Gold Coast and Nigerian governments. The firms became licensed buyers for the board on the Coast and were made responsible at first along with the London Office for the sale of cocoa on the world market. After the war the major contacts by business on Coast policy were mainly with the Gold Coast government and not with the Colonial Office.

The Boycott and disturbances in 1947 and 1948 again instigated meetings between the British firms and the government on the Coast, but not with the Colonial Office. The London representatives of UAC testified before the Commission on Disturbances in Accra but not in London. Prior to the war, because of time lags in communications, the colonial administration had handled government business with little direction from the Colonial Office. Now, despite improved communications, the Colonial Office would encourage the movement for self-government and thus release its hold on colonial affairs. The London Office soon after the war offered its assistance in working toward self-government and the establishment of cooperatives and trade unions, and proffered technical advice on problems of economic development.

British business in West Africa sometimes made its technical knowledge available to the local governments by serving as agents for the Cocoa Marketing Board, at other times waiting until government policies were established to determine its place in the new structure. Business, except through representation on the Legislative Council before independence and afterward through election of the Chamber of Commerce to two or three seats in the Assembly, held no regular place as an adviser on economic development. Business generally made presentations to the government and decided on the kinds of services they could give to the economy under conditions established by the government.

The firms were not consulted by the Coast government about specific development programs unless they had been directly involved in the economic activity under consideration, as with the marketing of cocoa. Testimony was taken in regard to mining concessions and the relation of the concerns to governmental participation. The firms were redeploying their resources by the sixties according to their understanding of government programs and policy. Some consultation on particular economic programs and problems continued between government and business management which had been associated with the Ghanaian economy for a long time, but still government did not make use of business consultation on any regular basis. Such consultation occured only after the NLC establishment of an economic committee and then, in the best known instance, with a former civil servant who had become a director of one of the mining concerns, and Minister of Trade and Industry in Busia's government.

Scholarships and Training, Redeploying Resources, Technical Assistance. The firms instituted scholarship funds and introduced programs for increasing the numbers of their African personnel. Cadburys had a long history, going back to the twenties, of supporting secondary schools and then, in the thirties, scholarship programs for the indigenous population. UAC began in the forties to support scholarship programs. There had been two impetuses for Africanisation of the civil service—the first in the twenties under Gordon Guggisberg and the second in the early forties under Sir Alan Burns. Some managers of firms associated with UAC in the Gold Coast in the twenties were Africans, but their numbers dwindled during the late thirties until UAC again began training some personnel on the job. The major programs of Africanisation in UAC and Cadburys began after World War Two and were enlarged during the fifties, at which time the Chamber of Mines and CAST also established training schools and other management training programs. The banks began to emphasize Africanisation in the sixties. The government seemed to exert little if any pressure for such programs on the British firms.

John Holt and Company came into the West African cocoa trade late and had just established itself as a cocoa-buying agent by the 1936-37 season. The cocoa Hold-Up occurred in the next season, and by 1940 Holts had begun to withdraw gradually from the Ghanaian market and redeploy its remaining resources in other activities until independence, when except for its motor activities, it withdrew entirely. During the fifties the company did provide some training opportunities for managers but never as active in either economic affairs or the development programs of the Coast as was the longer-standing merchant company, UAC, and the cocoa manufacturers, Cadburys.

UAC, formed as the result of a merger in 1929 of several long-standing merchant companies, was a major buyer of cocoa in the thirties and was in large part responsible for initiating the 1937 cocoa-marketing agreement between the British buying companies and manufacturers. This agreement was the impetus for major changes in cocoa-marketing procedures finally realized in 1947. Some Africanisation was supported by UAC in the later thirties through training opportunities on the managerial level, but the major programs were not established until the later forties and fifties. UAC sponsored scholarships and also redeployed its resources in the fifties and sixties. The company demonstrated the usual attitude of business toward government change—namely, to wait for government policy and then to adjust business activities according to the resources of the company. Directors of UAC and Unilever were able to maintain communications with Ghanaian leaders, and Nkrumah called upon them to assist with the operation of some of the plants built by other concerns. The economic committee of the NLC also maintained contact with UAC and consulted on problems of mutal interest.

Cadburys, except for the period when it was involved as a signatory of the 1937 Agreement, has enjoyed a very favorable reputation among the farmers and with the colonial and independent governments. Since the early thirties it has made presentations concerned with the quality of cocoa raised on the Coast and has promoted community interests through scholarship and community center activities and through consultations with the government over problems of cocoa farming and marketing. These activities have continued through each change of government.

Mining and banking concerns, by the mid-sixties, were providing training programs for middle-management positions. CAST led the way with its program for top management positions.

The Firms' Capacity to Accelerate Contributions. The economic development and progress toward political independence were so tightly interwoven in Ghana that it is difficult to separate them. Efforts and conditions that fostered economic development in many ways prepared the ground for political independence. Training for business positions, the improvement of secondary schools and universities, and the development of communication networks aided both economic and political progress.

The traditional basis of a market economy had been implanted in the Gold Coast by the 1930's. The rural, village-based economy, with the development of mineral resources, rapidly changed to a marketing process economy which culminated in new urban styles of life. These processes were changed by the British firms: cocoa manufacturing and merchandise and mining interests.

The establishment of manufacturing enterprises and of indigenous commercial concerns on the Coast also went hand in hand with the requirements for trained personnel. The encouragement of such enterprises through firms' actions presupposes the existence of educational and training facilities. It was only with increased facilities after the War and again with independence that indigenous personnel became visible. Cadburys as early as the twenties supported increased secondary opportunities, and each firm afforded either scholarships (Cadburys in the thirties) or training (UAC late thirties) to a much greater degree as the push for self-government moved ahead in the forties. The Colonial government had also supported more educational facilities in the twenties and during the thirties, but only after the war were they available to any significant degree, and with independence they became more adequate.

Certainly in Great Britain the push for educational and training facilities had come from the government, not from economic enterprises; it would therefore be unrealistic to expect that the firms would have pushed the Coastal government in these areas during the twenties and thirties. But by the mid-forties the Colonial Office, through Creech-Jones, was actively supporting more adequate educational and training facilities on the Coast, and the leaders of the indigenous population were also expecting increases in these facilities as they pushed for local self-government.

The firms, despite their reluctance to initiate programs other than those directly related to their specific activities, and despite their habit of waiting for a political change[1] before deciding on an appropriate economic response, contributed to the transfer of marketing institutions to the Coast. The firms could, at worst, be accused of riding the tide.

The Cocoa Farmer, the Marketing Board, and the International Market. The firms had sold cocoa on the world terminal markets in London and the United States and had thus participated in the markets' development. A number of the new nations—those mainly dependent on one or two cash crops for international exchange, including Ghana—found in the 1960's that the stability of their internal political structure was heavily dependent on world prices for their produce. In some instances national political institutions had not had time to develop enough stability to weather an economic crisis; Ghana is a good example. When the price of cocoa on the world market fell, internal crises of both political and economic accommodation occurred—as in the buying seasons beginning in 1937, 1965, and 1971. The infrastructure of the nation was not yet strong enough, nor were its political mores firmly enough established, to withstand the problems of high prices, unemployment, and loss of money to the farmer and country. Despite efforts to establish a national marketing-board structure for cocoa similar to the more successful models of the New Zealand dairy and meat boards, these problems contine to plague the Ghanaian nation.[2]

Since the International Cocoa Agreement became operative in 1973, despite the absence of certain manufacturing countries like the United States it has been possible to bring more stability to the world market through the International Cocoa Organisation, now based in London. Because the price of cocoa has been high, the full effect of the Organization is not yet known.

The farmers should have been provided with detailed knowledge of the international market. The Cocoa Marketing Boards had the potential to make such knowledge available. It will be interesting to see if the Ministry of Cocoa Affairs (formed in February 1975) involves the farmers more fully in marketing operations.

One function for cocoa marketing boards in Ghana, besides buying cocoa from the farmer and selling it on international markets, was to include representatives of the farmers on the Board, and thus to give the farmers a role in making decisions that affected their livelihood. Another function was to act in the interest of the farmer, to assist him to receive the best price for his goods.

Has the farmer, at any time during the century, understood the international market well enough to evaluate the fairness of his cocoa prices? It is probable that this information has never been complete enough. Often he has judged on the basis of the previous year's prices and information gleaned from various local sources. In 1937, when prices fell, he followed the advice of the chiefs, and in 1965 he again questioned the reliability of the government.

For the farmer to participate usefully in the Board's decision, he must be kept informed about the operations of the international market. Today this means knowledge about the internal market, about costs of internal purchase, about at least three national marketing arrangements (marketing boards, stabilization of prices and controls, and private enterprise controls), and about international marketing arrangements, including the futures market and the terminal markets. Throughout the Cocoa Marketing Board's life from 1947 to 1975, it is not clear that the farmer had adequate information nor, in turn, significant influence over the Board's operations.

Certainly the farmers, who reacted more strongly to price fluctuations and to lower farm prices than to international prices, should have had information about real costs of administration for buying, transportation of cocoa and for governmental use of cocoa funds. It seems clear that the farmers did not have such information before the Board's establishment, nor did these sources of information become adequate under the Boards. Ministerial control does not necessarily bring this information any closer to the farmer.

NOTES

Preface

1. J. P. D. Stewart, *British Pressure Groups* (London, Oxford University Press, 1958).
2. S. E. Finer, *Private Industry and Political Power* (London, Pall Mall, 1958). Graham Wootton, *Workers, Unions and the State* (London, Routledge and Kegan Paul, 1966). J. W. Grove, *Government and Industry* (London, Longmans Green, 1962). Samuel Beer, *Modern British Politics* (London, Faber, 1965). H. Eckstein, *Pressure Group Politics* (London, George Allen and Unwin, 1950). R. Rose, ed., *Policy Making in Britain* (London, Macmillan, 1969).
3. The records of UAC not as well organized as those of the two other firms. Fortunately, individuals connected with all firms have maintained some records in England and in Ghana. The family firm of John Holt had a fine archive system, including materials from the first days of the firm. These records were available to me in Liverpool. Recently, however, a large portion of Holts archives were transferred to Rhodes House, Oxford. Cadburys gave me access to its West Africa Committee proceedings in the Bournville office. These records cover the whole period emphasized in this volume. In addition, the personal files of John Cadbury, the firm's representative in the Gold Coast crisis of 1937-38, were generously shared. W. R. Feaver, the firm's representative on the Coast and later Director of the West African section, gave frequent advice on the location of source materials and described the firm's activities throughout the period covered by this volume.

1. The Approach and the Background

1. Lenin, *Imperialism* (New York, Vanguard Press, 1926) pp. 52, 83, 93. J. A. Hobson, *Imperialism* (New York, James Pott, 1902), p. 53.
2. See Kwame Nkrumah, *Neo-Colonialism* (London, Thomas Nelson, 1965), pp. 52-53, 69, 176. Bob Fitch and Mary Oppenheimer, *Ghana: End of an Illusion* (New York, Monthly Review Press, 1966).
3. *Unity or Poverty?* (Harmondsworth, England, Penguin Books, 1968), pp. 110-111. Cf. Reginald H. Green and Ann W. Seidman, *Economic Logic of African Unity* (Baltimore, Maryland, Penguin Books, 1968), pp. 22-23.
4. Interview, "Two Ways to Grow", *New York Times* (January 29, 1971), p. C.56.
5. Ibid.
6. C. H. Wilson, *The History of Unilever* (London, Cassell, 1954), Vol. 2, Part III, ch. 2. "The History of UAC to 1938", UAC Files, typescript (1938), pp. 137, 321-323. Bank of British West Africa, "Trade Report" (February 15, 1938), p 981.
7. *Merchant Adventure* (Northampton, Clerke and Sherwell, n.d., 1955), p. 16. Interviews with officials of Holts, December 1965.
8. Ibid., p. 16.

9. A survey of the cocoa trade was made in 1907, and Cadbury operations began in 1908. See Cadbury's publication *Our 50 Years in the Gold Coast and Ghana, 1907-1957* (Birmingham, 1958, mimcographed), and Cadbury's British West Africa Committee, *Records,* September 1936 (archives of Cadburys).

10. Consolidated African Selection Trust Limited (Akwatia, Ghana),. "Memorandum for Submission to Concession Commission of Enquiry, 1958", in CAST office in London, pp. 2, 5.

11. Question in Parliament April 30, 1917, by Mr. Trevelyan and answered by Mr. Long. See Cartland Papers. Also in the same papers are included extracts from enclosure I to Gold Coast Conference, October 10, 1931, and "General Considerations of Birim District", 1937-38.

12. Other business federations formed in Britain over the last fifty years have shown little concern for economic activities in West Africa. These include the former Federation of British Industries, the Commonwealth Industries Association, and the Association of British Chambers of Commerce. The Federation of British Industries, since 1965 the Confederation of British Industries (both hereafter referred to as CBI), is a national organization that has gained much prestige in governmental circles since World War II. The CBI has had little say in Gold Coast/Ghanaian politics, primarily because the Gold Coast involves mainly a producer market while CBI largely acts to bring manufacturing concerns together. In addition, CBI's policies in the past have evolved mainly from affairs of concern to the whole, diverse' membership and have thus taken the form of general statements that do not deal with special problem areas. A major area of concern for the CBI since the 1950's has been British membership in the European Common Market (EEC), but there was no mention of the possible effects on Ghanaian affairs, or, for that matter, on West African affairs. Another major function of the Confederation has been to give advice to its membership about proposed expansions and about problems involving governmental contracts. Thus a great deal of the CBI's day-to-day governmental contact is through the Board of Trade. Since World War II some of the directors of the Confederation have in fact acted in a semipublic capacity by helping the government to negotiate certain trade arrangements with other countries. CBI sponsors trade missions to various parts of the world, and during recent years some of the administrative staff have passed through Ghana, but there have been no missions as such because, for the manufacturers, Ghana has not presented as much promise of expansion as have other parts of the world. (Interviews with officers of the Confederation of British Industries and with Peter Mathias, Cambridge University, Autumn 1965. Also CBI, *Annual Reports.*)

The CBI has seldom acted on behalf of its members' interest in West African affairs or made official contact with the Colonial Office. The few members who do have an interest in West Africa have, on almost all occasions. made their own contacts. As each colony has become independent, business contacts with the Colonial Office have become less and less frequent, and contacts with the local governments and perhaps at times with the former Ministry of Overseas Development have increased.

A few other British federations should be mentioned, even though their contacts with governmental offices on West African affairs have been fewer than those of the CBI. The Commonwealth Industries Association was formed in 1947 and has served mainly as a propaganda agency for members of parliament. (Commonwealth Industries Association, "Information Sheet", 1966. The CIA was founded in 1926 under the title Empire Industries Association. In 1947 it merged with the British Empire League, formed in 1895, to establish the CIA. Sources also include annual reports, the *Monthly Bulletin,* and interviews with the General Secretary in 1965 and 1966.) Even though the CIA claims to be nonpartisan, its programs tend to favor the Conservative Party's attitudes more than Labour's. The Institute of Directors and the Association of the British Chambers of Commerce, again as groups, have had little concern for West African affairs.

13. Joint West Africa Committee, Records, located in London and in Holts files; and interviews with the General Secretary and Directors in Spring of 1966.

14. Joint West Africa Committee, Minutes, located in the London office; and letter from W. T. Gates, Holts, April 1966.

15. The term AWAM, from the thirties, was popularly associated with shortages and price fixing on the Coast; hence the hostility toward AWAM in the late forties was a continuation of this popular concept of the Association as "coney-coney."

16. J. C. de Graft-Johnson. "The Population of Ghana 1846-1967", *Transactions of the Historical Society of Ghana,* 10 (1969), 1-12. William A. Hance, *Population Migration and Urbanization in Africa* (New York, Columbia University Press, 1970), pp. 222-224. John Caldwell, *African Rural-Urban Migration: The Movement to Ghana's Towns* (New York, Columbia University Press, 1969). Among sources used in this chapter on the political, economic, and social history of Ghana are W. K. Hancock, *Survey of the British Commonwealth: Problems of Economic Policy,* Vol. 2, Part II (London, Oxford University Press, 1942); Michael Crowder, *West Africa under Colonial Rule* (London, Hutchinson, 1968), pp. 335-342; F. M. Bourret, *Ghana: The Road to Independence, 1919-1957* (Stanford, Stanford University Press, 1960); L. H. Gann and Peter Duignan, eds., *Colonialism in Africa, 1914-1960,* Vol. 2 (Cambridge, Cambridge University Press, 1970); David Kimble, *A Political History of Ghana, 1850-1928* (Oxford, Clarendon Press, 1963); Lord Hailey, *An African Survey* (London, Oxford University Press, 1938); Dennis Austin, *Politics in Ghana* (London, Oxford University Press, 1964), pp. 13-17, 48; and J. F. A. Ajayi and Michael Crowder, eds., *History of West Africa,* Vol. 2 (London, Longmans, 1974) pp. 514-541.

17. Bourret, pp. 13-17, 48. J. D. Fage, *A History of West Africa* (Cambridge, Cambridge University Press 1969), pp. 69, 168-469. Hancock, pp. 201-210. Unofficial historian, "The History of the United Africa Company Limited to 1938", UAC files, 1938, typescript.

18. Bourret, p. 16. Fage, pp. 69, 74, 126-130.

19. Fage, pp. 167-169.

20. Bourret, pp. 18-20, 37. Austin, pp. 1-10. Commission of Enquiry into Disturbances in the Gold Coast, *Report,* 1948 (London. HMSO), Colonial No. 231, p. 101.

21. Crowder, pp. 3, 203. Austin, p. 8.
22. Bourret, pp. 22, 117-118. Fage, pp. 205-209. Interviews with Sir Alan Burns, 1965 and 1966.
23. Royal Commission on the Marketing of West African Cocoa, *Report* (London, HMPO, 1938), Cmd. 5845.
24.

Table 12

Urban Population in Ghana					
	%		*Population in Accra, 1901-1966*		
1921	8.7	1901	27,000	1948	136,000
1948	14.35	1911	30,000	1960	492,000
1960	21.65	1921	43,000	1966	600,000
		1931	60,000		

Sources: Hance, pp. 238-239, and Crowder, pp. 335 ff.

25. Crowder, pp. 274, 284, 288, 372-389. Hailey, passim. Bourret, esp. pp. 131-141. On inflation see also *United Nations Statistical Yearbooks, 1964, 1972; Statistical Abstract for the United Kingdom from 1913 to 1927* (January 1929), p. 95; and *Britain, An Official Handbook* (various editions, including 1968), p. 245. Information about incomes and consumer indexes is most difficult to evaluate for developing nations, particularly for a society that is predominately agricultural. The British figures have therefore been used when they are available, as the income on the Coast was tied to the British. See Colin Clark for information on incomes from the 1830 to 1936 period, *National Income and Outlay* (London, Frank Cass, 1966), p. 233; and for incomes and indexes in developing nations, Colin Clark and Margaret Haswell, *The Economics of Subsistence Agriculture* (London, Macmillan, 4th edition, 1970), pp. 172-190. Also Colin Clark, *The Conditions of Economic Progress* (London, Macmillan, 3rd ed., 1960), international units for advanced countries (1938), pp. 18-19, 31-33, and oriental units for developing countries, pp. 31-33.
26. Table for Crowder, pp. 325, 310, 325.
27. Crowder, pp. 325.
28. After the Second World War, development funds were not allotted in large part to the Gold Coast. Among the reasons for the little support from this fund apparently was the poor relations between the director of the fund and the governor. Interview with a former colonial official, April 1966.
29. Bourret, pp. 28-31. Fage, p. 188.
30. Kimble, p. 52. See also Royal Commission on the Marketing of West African Cocoa, *Report* (London, HMSO, 1938), Cmd. 5845. Information on cocoa exports from Ghana appear in Bourret, p. 233; Hancock, p. 209; and Ghana, Cocoa Marketing Board, *Report* (1965).

2. The 1938 Cocoa Crises

1. W. K. Hancock, *Survey of British Commonwealth Affairs*, Vol. 2, Part II, pp. 212-213.

2. Sam Rhodie, "The Gold Coast Cocoa Hold-Up of 1930-31",
    Transactions of the Historical Society of Ghana, 9 (1968), 103-118.
3. Kimble, *A Political History of Ghana,* pp. 48, 45. See also Crowder, *West
    Africa Under Colonial Rule,* pp. 66-67, and Hancock, pp. 212-220.
4. Kimble, pp. 45 ff.
5. Freda Wolfson, "A Price Agreement on the Gold Coast—The Krobo
    Oil Boycott, 1858-1866", *Economic History Review,* 6 (1953), 68-83.
    Hancock pp. 223-225. Commission on the Marketing of West African
    Cocoa, *Report* (London, September 1938), Cmd. 5845.
6. George H. T. Kimble, *Tropical Africa,* Vol. 1, *Land and Livelihood* (New
    York, Twentieth Century Fund, 1960), pp. 137-162. Polly Hill, *Studies
    in Rural Capitalism in West Africa* (Cambridge, Cambridge University
    Press, 1970), pp. 21-29.
7. Hancock, pp. 212-213.
8. Ibid., pp. 2, 3, 216.
9. Ibid., p. 216; Commission on the Marketing of West African Cocoa,
    Report (London 1938), Cmd. 5845, pp. 124-129. S. L. Hale, in T. K.
    Warley, ed., *Agricultural Producers and Their Markets* (Oxford, Basil
    Blackwell, 1967), pp. 142-145.
10. Hancock, pp. 212 ff and Commission Report. Interviews, including W.
    T. Beckett's, July 1968.
11. Hancock, p. 338. Bourret, p. 66. Kimble, pp. 30-37. Polly Hill's *Migrant
    Cocoa Farmers of Southern Ghana* (Cambridge, Cambridge University
    Press, 1963) is an extraordinarily useful background source for an
    understanding of the development of cocoa farming.
12. Wilson, *History of Unilever,* Vol. 2, Part III, chap. 2. *"The History of
    UAC to 1938,"* pp. 137, 321-323. *Trade Report,* Bank of British West
    Africa (February 15, 1938), p. 981. *Merchant Adventure,* published for
    Holts (1955), p. 16. Interview with officials from Holts, December 1965.
    A survey of the cocoa trade was made in 1907, and Cadbury operations
    began in 1908. See *Our 50 Years in the Gold Coast and Ghana 1907-1957*
    (Birmingham, Cadbury Brothers, 1958); BWA, Cadburys, and British
    West Africa Committee (BWA) Records (September 1936); and Cmd.
    5845, pp. 50, 57-58.
13. C. N. Hunt, "Justification of the Agreement," March 1938, in Holts
    Records. Communication from Nsawan, March 17, 1938, in Holts
    Records. Cadburys Records, June 1937.
14. Cadburys records, Report of meeting with Lyons, July 1937.
15. Ibid., August 1937.
16. Cmd. 5845, pp. 50, 54-58. Records of the firms indicate that all
    signatures were not obtained for the agreement until November; see
    Cadburys collection.
17. Ibid., Cadburys Records, September 1937 and October 1937, both
    letters in UAC and Cadburys records. See also CMD. 5845, pp. 50, 54-
    58.
18. John Cadbury and Frank Samuel, letter to Colonial Office (Sir Cecil
    Bottomley), September 27, 1937; and letter to Mr. Samuel, October 7,
    1937. Sources for material are UAC and Cadburys Records.
19. John Cadbury and Frank Samuel, letters, Cadburys Records,
    September 1937 and October 1937.

20. C. N. Hunt, "Justification of the Agreement", March 1938, in Holts Records. Memorandum: Communications from Nsawan, March 17, 1938, in Holts Records.
21. Letters, September 27, 1937, and October 7, 1937.
22. Ibid.
23. Cadburys Records, October 1937.
24. Cmd. 5845, pp. 50, 54-58. Records of the firms indicate that all signatures were not obtained for the agreement until November; see Cadburys collection.
25. "Justification of the Agreement", March 1938. Memorandum: Communication from Nsawan, March 17, 1938, in Holts Records.
26. UAC Records, October 1938.
27. Ibid., pp. 50, 57-58.
28. Liverpool Chamber of Commerce, Minutes of West African Section, 1939, pp. 79-80; 1938, pp. 76, 79; 1939, pp. 71, 75.
29. See above, p 5, and note 12.
30. John Cadbury, "Report on Visit to Gold Coast" (typescript in his Collection, 1938), p. 7.
31. Ibid., p. 1. Manufacturing firms, "Statement to the Cocoa Enquiry Commission" (London, May 30, 1938), p. 5.
32. UAC records and Holts Records, December 1938.
33. CMD. 5845, p. 1.
34. Holts Records, March 1938.
35. Unofficial historian, "The History of UAC to 1938", UAC Records Trade Bank of BWA, February 15, 1938, pp. 147-148.
36. "The History of UAC to 1938."
37. Ibid.
38. Among the Akan, Ashanti, and other groups the stool is the symbol of a chief's authority and legitimacy. On the rare occasions when a chief loses favor, he can be deposed—that is destooled.
39. Report filed, Government Archives, Accra, 1937
40. See *Birmingham Daily Post,* October 30, 1937; *New Chronicle,* November 11, 1937; *Public Ledger,* October 30 and November 1, 1937; and *Echo,* October 9, 1937.
41. *West Africa* (September 18, 1937), p. 1238. Columnists in the Gold Coast frequently used pseudonyms for their regular contributions. "Anokwalefo" means truthteller, and "Osampa" means true story.
42. See above, p. 12.
43. Cable, reported in John Cadbury's Collection and in UAC *Records,* December 1937.
44. Cable, reported in John Cadbury's Collection. The farmers had very little organization before the Hold-Up. Chiefs sanctioned the Hold-Up but had no way of preventing the people from selling. Chiefs seemed to back the people, thus maintaining the Hold-Up. Interview with Sir George Sinclair (Secretary to Governor in 1938), July 1967.
45. Cable, reported in John Cadbury's Collection.
46. Firms (UAC, Cadburys and Holts) *Records,* December 6, 7, 9, 1937, and January 1938 (3 items).
47. UAC *Records,* December 1937.
48. Cmd. 5845, p. 1.

49. Minutes of General Committee (G. C. Cocoa Scheme), London, February 23, 1938, (Holts Records).
50. Holts Records, March 1938.
51. Ibid.
52. Proceedings of the Council meeting, March 10, 1938, Holts Records. See also testimony from Holts to the Commission of Enquiry.
53. Holts Records, letters, April 1938. Interview with Sir George Sinclair, July 1967. Holts Records, February 1938 and April 1938. Interview I. K. Agyeman, July 1966.
55. Holts Records, April 1938, Letter from A. R. I. Mellor to F. Samuel, April 21, 1938.
56. Holts Records, letters, April 1938. Interview, Sir George Sinclair, July 1967. Interview, I. K. Agyeman, July 1966.
57. *Manchester Guardian,* October 25, 1938. See also below note 71, for 1936-38 prices and sales.
58. Ibid., October 25, 1938.
59. "State of Evidence to be given to the Cocoa Commission by Mr. F. Samuel of the United Africa Company Ltd, and Mr. John Cadbury of Cadbury Brothers Ltd, June 2, 1938," John Cadbury Collection, typescript, pp. 9-10.
60. Ibid. Wolfson, "Price Agreement on the Gold Coast" pp. 68-83.
61. "Précis of evidence to be given by Mr. Jasper W. Knight (UAC) June 8, 1938," typescript in John Cadbury's Collection. Describes the Cocoa Marketing Company. See also report 8 in the same collection.
62. "State of the manufacturing firms who have buying agencies in British West Africa and who are parties to the Buying Agreement," Cadbury, J. S. Fry, Cadbury and Fry, and J. Lyons, typescript forwarded on May 30, 1938, John Cadbury's Collection.
63. *Manchester Guardian,* October 25, 1938.
64. Ibid., November 00, 1938.
65. Holts *Records,* October 9, 1938.
66. Ibid., August 00, 1938.
67. Firms (UAC, Cadburys, and Holts) *Records,* January 1939. According to the records, no further agreements were made after the Commission Report. The last reference affirming that no agreement or understanding between the parties to the cocoa agreement had been made after its abondonment in November 1939 is in a cable from Frank Samuels to the Sachs Commission in November 1947.
68. Firms *Records,* February 1939.
69. The two committees reported to the Governor in the spring of 1939 in time for the Secretary of State for the Colonies to comment on May 23 in the Commons concerning a preliminary examination of the reports, and to state that no modification of marketing was thought possible in respect to the 1939-40 crop. See Ghana National Government Archives for the Reports Rhodes House, Oxford. Mr. Emory's Minority Report to the Accra Committee Report is also located at Rhodes House. See also below, pp. 45–46, for a more detailed description of the committee reports.
70. A despatch from the Governor indicated on November 26 that "the world price of cocoa is determined primarily by the New York market and to a lesser degree by the European market...."; quoted in *The Times,*

March 25, 1938. In the UAC yearly report the fluctuation of coca prices was also explained: "With the commencement of the company's financial year (October 1), the value of Gold Coast cocoa for the new crop was approximately £35 per ton. At the height of the season, on January 18, it had risen to £58 10s. per ton, and at the close of the financial year it had fallen to £30 per ton. Since that date it has been as low as £23 per ton, while at the present value is in the neighbourhood of £28-£29 per ton." It was estimated that there were about 200,000 cocoa farmers at that time, and they were thought to stand a greater loss than the chiefs and the brokers. *The Times,* March 28, 1938.

71. Other quotes include the one on cocoa and cotton on March 12, 1938:

	Jan.	Dec.
	£ s. d.	£ s. d.
Accra cocoa	55 7 0	25 6 0
Palm oil (softs)	29 5 0	16 3 0
Copra	23 5 0	14 3 0
Palm kernels	18 3 0	11 2 0
Ground nuts, Nigerian	16 2 0	12 1 0

Manchester Guardian, March 12, 1938.

Supplies had reached their highest level in the 1936-37 season: "According to the 'Gordian', world supplies (or more strictly, world net exports) reached 718,739 metric tons in 1936-37, i.e. nearly 13,000 metric tons more than in the preceding season and a new all-time record." *Financial Times,* January 3, 1938. A composite figure, then, for the world price of cocoa was £29 4s 0d., and on this basis the price to the farmer was £14 4s 0d. during the 1937-38 season. Quoted by J. B. Wills (below).

Table 13.   COCOA PRICES

Year	World Price (£ per ton)	Price to the Farmer	
		(£ per ton)	(s. per load = 60 lb)
1937-38	29.4	14.4	7s. 6d*
1945-46	49.8	27.0	14s. 6d
1946-47	155.0	51.3	27s. 6d
1947-48	238.0	74.7	40s. –
1948-49	139.0	121.3	65s. –
1949-50	190.0	84.0	45s. –
1950-51	208.0	130.7	70s. –
1951-52	285.0	148.3	80s. –
1952-53	301.0	130.7	70s. –

*S. La Anyane reports this price for Oda; the price from Accra was 8s. See J. B. Wills, ed., *Agriculture and Land Use in Ghana* (London, Oxford University Press 1962), p. 199; and Dennis Austin, *Politics in Ghana 1946-60* (London, Oxford University Press, 1964), p. 157. The price to the farmers was estimated in a Memorandum a to the Colonial Office on April 22, 1938, from the buying firms. See also below, p. 135, note 6.

72. Minutes of the West Africa Committee (London Office).

73. Most of the Colonial Service was staffed by people who had undertaken the traditional courses at Oxford and Cambridge. This study included little if anything about economics until the Second World War.
74. Interview with Sir George Sinclair, July 1967.
75. A. G. Hopkins, "Economic Aspects of Political Movements in Nigeria and the Gold Coast, 1918-1939," *Journal of African History,* 7 (1966). See also Wolfson and Rhodie (above, p.131, notes 5, 2).
76. John Cadbury, interview. Cadburys Committee on West Africa, *Minutes.*

3. Wartime Controls and Cocoa Marketing

1. The effects of World War II on Ghanaian development is the focus of several works about Ghanaian economic and political affairs. Bauer, on West African trade, pp. 246-259, presents a critical analysis of governmental arrangements. Bourret, pp. 142-166, gives the economic and political background, and Austin, pp. 3-11 discusses the war in connection with the political repercussions following it:
2. Hopkins, pp. 151-152.
3. Fage, pp. 203-206. Bourret, pp. 142-156, Crowder, pp. 482, 492 ff.
4. Michael Crowder, "The 1939-45 War and West Africa," in Ajayi and Crowder, pp. 596-621, esp. pp. 608-614.
5. *Gold Coast Gazette,* December 12, 1939; Regulations under the Emergency Power (Defense) Act 1939, no. 5 of 1940, in Holts file 421A, now located at Rhodes House, Oxford. Types of produce are listed in the reports of Martindale (Gold Coast, "Report of Enquiry into the Conduct and Management of the Supplies and Customs Departments," Accra, 1947) and Sachs (Gold Coast, "Report of Enquiry Repudiating Allegations in the report of the Commission of Enquiry into the Conduct and Management of the Supplies and Customs Departments," Accra, 1948). See also Bauer, pp. 81-85, and the A. C. Miles Papers, now at Rhodes House.
6. Letter from Rawlings to Goddard, September 18, 1939. Holts file 536ii.
7. Nigeria, November 1939; see Holts file 421.
8. Ibid., Holts memorandum, February 26, 1940. Interview Sir Eric Tansley, February 16, 1966. Government allowed only 2 percent on cocoa trade.
9. Sixth Meeting of the Central Control Office, November 30, 1939, Holts file 421A (i); reported in December 5, 1939.
10. This section is based on interviews with John Cadbury and W. R. Feaver, 1966, 1967, and July 24, 1968; and Sir Eric Tansley and Mr. E. Byle, February 16 and June 1966.
11. See interviews with John Cadbury, November 1965 and August 1966. Also Colonial Office and Ministry of Food records.
12. See *Report on Cocoa Control in West Africa, 1939-1943,* Cmd. 6554, A20, 23. Interview, Sir Eric Tansley, February 16, 1966, and Mr. E. Byle, June 1966.
13. Cadburys, BWA, Minutes, November 13, 1939.
14. Ibid., 1944-1949, 71e and 79e, January 30, 1947.

15. Minutes of the British West Africa Committee, Cadburys, July 7, 1938 ff. Cadburys Records are located in Office Records in Cadburys Bournville offices.
16. Communication from John Cadbury, Director of British West African Cocoa Controls, December 22, 1939, in Holts Records, file 536.
17. Ibid., Cadburys files, May 1940, and letter outlining minutes from A. P. Williamson, November 1967, in a report written in May 1940, by the West African Committee.
18. November 15, 1939, Holts file 536.
19. It is of interest to note that this was a route similar to that taken by the slave-trading vessels of the previous centries.
20. Mr. MacDonald's statement on price policy for purchase of Gold Coast Cocoa crop in the House of Commons, reviewed in *West Africa* (March 2, 1940), p. 178; and Hansard, House of Commons, March 31, 1944.
21 This and the following material is based on interviews with Coast governmental officials, including W. H. Beckett, July 16, 1968.
22. Beckett estimated that he essentially drew up a list in one morning.
23. Beckett, July 16, 1968.
24. Bauer, pp. 115-116, 203 ff. Leventis had worked with G. B. Ollivant for sixteen years. In March 1938 he began his own company, which was incorporated under Gold Coast laws in March 1940. Leventis did export cocoa in 1938.
25. Interviews with Sir Eric Tansley, January 1966, and W. H. Beckett, July 16, 1968. See also Charlotte Lenbuscher, *The West African Shipping Trade, 1909-1959* (Leyden: A. W. Sythoff, 1963).
26. *Records,* July 13, 1942, p. 3. Sir Eric Tansley, interview, February 16, 1966.
27. *Records,* December 14, 1942. Ibid., and Beckett, interview, July 16, 1968.
28. Interviews (above notes 10, 11, 22, 25).
29. See records of these groups (note 15, above and Holts, 1939-1945).
30. A. Hopkins (note 2, above), pp. 151-152, for one interpretation.
31. Bauer, pp. 280-286.
32. Bourret; Bauer, pp. 246-259.
33. Ibid., and Tony Killick in Walter Birmingham, et al., *A Study of Contemporary Ghana* (London: George Allen and Unwin, 1966), pp. 365-371.
34. Sir Eric Tansley, interview, February 16, 1966. W. H. Beckett, interview 16 July 1968. Prices of cocoa to the farmer and on the world market were between £16 and £18 per ton during the war, and in 1945-46 £27 per ton. See above, note 20, and Dennis Austin, *Politics in Ghana* (Oxford, 1964), pp. 5, 157.
35. Interviews with Sir Alan Burns, 1965, 1966, and comments on transcript, 1970.
36. Discussion of quotas and the Group B shippers, for instance, occupied a large portion of a meeting of 'A' shippers in 1944: "Meeting of Gold Coast 'A' Shipper Members of AWAM held at Unilever House, E.C.4. 31st May 1944"; minutes in Holts Records, file 536iii. Such discussions of the effect of the B shippers' inability to realize quotas could indicate efforts to restrict B shippers; yet the degree of exploitation in these discussions is certainly questionable and almost impossible to determine.

4. Plans for Postwar Cocoa Marketing

1. H. J. Rawlings, *"Cocoa Commission Report"* (November 1, 1938), p. 2-3.
2. Ibid., p. 2.
3. Ibid., p. 6.
4. Holts Records, letter from District Agent, Accra, entitled *"Cocoa Commissions Recommendations,"* February 6, 1939.
5. "Committee appointed by the Governor of the Gold Coast to Examine and Report on the Recommendations of the Cocoa Enquiry Commission," p. 19. See also *Morning Post,* December 17, 1938; *Liverpool Daily Post,* December 19, 1938; and interview Jack More, July 1966.
6. *Spectator Daily,* March 16, 23, 31, 1939, and interview, Jack More, July 1966.
7. F. G. Emery, "Minutes and Notes," Accra Committee, February 20–March 25, 1939, Rhodes House.
8. Ashanti (Kumasi) Committee, *Report.*
9. F. G. Emery, "Minority report, the Accra Committee Report" (above, note 7).
10. Above, note 4.
11. Letter from UAC dated April 17, 1939.
12. Cadburys Records, "Minutes of B. W. A. Committee," 1938-1946.
13. Cable from Frank Samuel of UAC to Office of the Special Commission, Accra, November 14, 1947. See also letters from Samuel in 1944 and 1946.
14. Secretary of State for the Colonies, *Report on Cocoa Control on West Africa,* London, HMSO Cmd. 6554 (September 1944), p. 11.
15. Ibid., pp. 11-12.
16. The Combined Food Board in Washington was established during World War II to control food imports.
17. Cmd 6554, p. 12.
18. Secretary of State for the Colonies, "Statement on Future Marketing of West African Cocoa," Cmd. 6950 (1946), p. 3.
19. Ibid., p. 5.
20. A. C. Miles notes. Files on Colonial Office conferences.
21. Holts, UAC, and Cadbury records on letters from Frank Samuel, November 10 and December 21, 1944.
22. Draft statement to representative of cocoa manufacturers, September 21, 1944. Notes on Meetings in Colonial Office, September 20, November 16 and 28, 1944.
23. Minutes, February 13, 1945.
24. Quoted in minutes.
25. Ibid.
26. A. C. Miles file on the report.
27. Yet criticisms of trading abuses by B shippers did arise. At a May 31, 1944, meeting of Gold Coast A shipper members of AWAM held at Unilever House, E.C.4, Mr. Samuel of UAC, who had recently been to the Gold Coast, reviewed the trading position on the Coast:

Conditions were chaotic. The existing Agreements regarding brokerages \ ere entirely disregarded and buying had become a scramble—everyone being out to buy the greatest quantity possible. There was no collaboration whatever between firms locally, only lip service being paid to the Agreements, and the general atmosphere gave one the impression of an almost complete return to the old time abuses. This state of affairs was most marked in the Eastern Province. As much as 18/- per ton commission had been paid in some cases. He was told that the trouble was started by the "B" Shippers. These people, who had had a collective quota of 28,500 tons, had only obtained 22,000 tons in the previous season and were afraid that if this shortfall continued their quotas would be So to obtain tonnage they grossly overpaid brokerages, and a number of "A" Shippers had been following suit in order to keep their own positions intact.

(Minutes of meeting in Holts Records, folder 536iii.)

28. For discussion of these questions see below, pp. 115-125. .

5. Postwar Dissension and Change, 1947-1948

1. Interview with W. H. Beckett, July 1968, and W. R. Feaver, July 1967.
2. See the Creech-Jones Papers in Rhodes House, Oxford, from 1937 to 1957, and the Volta River study of 1940. For more information about those documents, see interview with Basil Bolt, New Zealand Foreign Office, July 1969. Bolt was formerly in the Colonial Service in Accra, 1946 ff.
3. F. M. Bourret, *Ghana* (Stanford, Stanford University Press, 1960), p. 169.
4. Ibid., pp. 168-170. Commission of Enquiry into Disturbances in the Gold Coast, 1948, *Report* (Colonial No. 231), p. 35. Austin, *Politics in Ghana*, pp. 49-69. David E. Apter, *The Gold Coast in Transition* (Princeton, Princeton University Press, 1955), pp. 164 f. Interviews with Sir Patrick FitzGerald, June 1966, and Lord Carrington, July 1967. See Colin Clark, *The Conditions of Economic Progress,* 3rd ed. (London, Macmillan, 1960), pp. 18-19, 31-33.
5. Gold Coast, Ordinance 16 of 1947. Gold Coast, *Legislative Council Debated* (March 20, 1947), pp. 156-167. Gold Coast Cocoa Marketing Board, *First Annual Report* (October 19, 1948), pp. 1-7. "Report of the Commission of Enquiry into the Affairs of the Cocoa Purchasing Company Ltd., Gold Coast" (1956), p. 1.
6. Report, West Africa Cocoa Marketing, September 1944, Cmd. 6554, pp. 3-6 13. Gold Marketing Board, *First Annual Report,* p. 3. £13 million was the amount of reserves turned over.
7. *See First Annual Report,* p. 3, and above, p. 136, note 34.
8. B. W. A. Committee Minutes, "General Manager's Report," July 5, 1944, to July 20, 1949. Vol. 2, Season 1947-48, p. 2.
9. Reports from the Gold Coast Press, 1946-48, in Sir George Cartland's Papers: "Criticisms of British Concerns in the West African Press, 1946-48," p. 7. Marketing Board's *Annual Reports,* 1947-66.

10. Gill and Duffus, Ltd., *Cocoa Statistics* (London, May 1964); and General Manager's Reports to B.W.A. Committee (1947-56), p. 35.
11. Gill and Duffus, pp. 8-9.
12. Cadbury and Fry, "The Cocoa, Chocolate and Confectionary Alliance, Ltd" (Accra, April 1, 1952), p. 8. Bourret, p. 206.
13. Paul S. Cadbury, "Report on a Visit to the Gold Coast, January 1956" (Accra, 1956), p. 13. Bourret, p. 206.
14. P. T. Bauer, *West African Trade* (2nd ed. London, Routledge and Kegan Paul, 1963), Parts V-VI. See also interview with Sir Eric Tansley, June 1, 1966; and Tony Killick, "Sectors of the economy: Cocoa," in Walter Birmingham, et al., *A Study of Contemporary Ghana* (London, George Allen and Unwin, 1966), Vol. 1, pp. 236-249.
15. Gold Coast, "Reports of Enquiry into the Conduct and Management of the Supplies and Customs Department" (Accra, 1947). Mr. Leventis became Ghana's first Ambassador to France.
16. Gold Coast, "Report of Enquiry Repudiating Allegations in the report of the Commission of Enquiry into the Conduct and Management of the Supplies and Customs Departments" (Accra, 1948).
17. Ibid., p. 67, par. 259.
18. Ibid., p. 68, par. 262.
19. Ibid., par. 269.
20. Ibid., p. 67, par. 261.
21. Interview with F. J. Pedler, February 1966.
22. See above, note 4. The following description of the march return indicates how little the disturbance was observed in some sections of Accra:

SIDELIGHTS ON THE RECENT CIVIL DISTURBANCE: WHICH OCCURRED IN ACCRA, CAPITAL OF THE G. C. ON 28TH FEB. 1948. BY AN EYEWITNESS *(n. d., in handwriting of W. H. A. Hanschell)*

(At the time of the riots a cricket match was being played on the Cricket Ground between two local sides: Europeans versus Africans. After the shots had been fired, the crowd, retreating from the nearby area of firing, approached the ground, by which time they had slackened to a fast walk. They started to walk across the pitch.)

Fortunately, however, the African players, who were fielding & who were all respectable citizens themselves, were able to turn them off the field by pointing out that "the" game was in progress; and this apparently did the trick, for they turned aside and passed along the outskirts of the field, thereby causing no trouble. . . . (While the author was fielding in the outfield, he saw 3 men chasing 3 looters. They captured one man and the loot.) They then marched back along the field and were going to pass between myself and the wicket when I drew their attention to the fact that the game was still in progress & they politely passed behind me, explaining at the same time that their prisoner was a "looter"!

Needless to say, not unlike other occasions in British history where momentous events have shown a tendency to interfere with our sporting traditions, we continued our game of cricket, which had not been interrupted for one moment by the afternoon's proceedings, & played out the match to a conclusion, which funnily enough resulted in a decisive win for the African side; and this whilst rioting and looting on a widespread and serious scale was taking place in the shopping centre of town (not more than 1/2 mile away) & of which we were quite oblivious at the time!

From Rhodes House, Oxford, MSS Afr. s.578 (W. H. A. Hanschell, *Gold Coast Notes, 1940-43*), fol. 138.

23. Interviews during 1966 with Sir Patrick FitzGerald (Manager, Accra, UAC), Peter Canham (Assistant Colonial Secretary), and others on the Coast in 1947-48,
24. "Report of the Commission of Enquiry into Disturbances on the Gold Coast" (1948), Colonial no. 231.
25. Ibid.
26. Ibid.
27. George Cartland Papers, "The Gold Coast Riots," pp. 2, 6.
28. Cartland Papers, "Criticisms of British Concerns in the West African Press, 1946-48," p.4.
29. Ibid., p. 1.
30. Letter dated January 4, 1948, in UAC files in the Ghana office.
31. R. I. Edwards, "Prices of Controlled Commodities in Retail Stores," (Accra, August 20, 1942), Cadburys' Records.
32. Interview with Lord Cole, February 1966; and this copy from *The Daily Echo,* April 1948, gives the UAC price list:

THE UNITED AFRICA COMPANY LIMITED.

AN ANNOUNCEMENT ON PRICES

All those who have the interests of the Gold Coast truly at heart will desire to see imported goods reaching the ultimate consumers at fair and reasonable prices. Under conditions of short supply, it is only natural that uncontrolled goods will ultimately be sold at the highest price they will fetch. The United Africa Company has not, and never has had, any desire to profit by the circumstances of the short supply of imported goods. Its branches have always had strict instructions not to exceed the controlled prices. The Company is anxious to play its part in assuring that those necessities of life in the Gold Coast, marketed by it, should reach the ultimate consumer at the lowest possible cost.

The Company has therefore decided, with effect from Saturday, 1st May, 1948, to put into force the following reduced prices:

Sugar, per lb.		7.
Evaporated milk, 6 oz. tins		6.
Corned beef, 12 oz. tins	1.	2.
Flour, 5 lbs. in bag	3.	5.
Flour, 50 lbs. in bag	31.	0.
Soap, pale, 3 lb. bar	1.	9.
Raft, 6006 Indian	18.	0.
„ 8888 Indian	18.	0.
White shirting, 6115 Mexican	25.	0.
Drill, 5010 D. 34 U.K.	24.	0.
„ 5452 T. 20 U.K.	24.	0.
„ 5458 U.K.	24.	0.
„ Achimola U.K.	25.	6.
„ 666314 German	27.	0.
„ 6843 American	7.	0.
„ 6869 Indian	28.	6.

Raleigh Cycles, standard, without special fittings	£11.	0.	0.
Other models will be subject to a similar reduction			
Cycle tyres, 28 × 1½, War grade		6.	0.
Cycle tubes, 28 × 1½,		2.	0.
Fishing nets—General reduction by one-ninth.			
Fishermen's Sisal ropes, per cod of 120 fathoms:			
1 inch circ.		38.	6.
1⅛ ,, ,,		41.	6.
1¼ ,, ,,		54.	0.
1½ ,, ,,		81.	6.
1¾ ,, ,,		100.	0.
Matchets, U.K., per doz.		24.	0.
,, each		2.	3.
Disc hoes per doz.		17.	0.
,, ,, each		1.	6.
Cement, British, in bags at port, per ton		170.	0.
Special prices for larger quantities of cement			
Nails per lb.			9.
Sewing cotton Star No. 40, per gross, White		100.	0.
Black		109.	0.
Colours		113.	0.
Anchor No. 10		122.	0.

This does not necessarily mean that large stocks of these commodities are now available at the Company's stores. What it does mean is that such stocks as the Company holds and stocks which are expected shortly will be sold from U. A. C. stores at the above prices, so long as there is no advance in the present cost at which these supplies are delivered. The Company appreciates fully that if the general mass of consumers is to reap any benefit from the new prices, there are others— Government, merchants, retailers, who must in turn, play their part. We call on everyone to co-operate loyally in showing that the Gold Coast feels a special responsibility to its people in keeping down the cost of the necessities of life.

33. I. K. Agyeman and others pointed out that Krobo Edusei was responsible for organizing the textile boycott of 1948 during this period (Austin, pp. 70 ff.). See also Commission of Enquiry, George Cole Testimony, April 30, 1948, in Ghana UAC files, pp. 5-7.
34. Commission of Enquiry, George Cole Testimony, p. 1.
35. Ibid., p. 2.
36. Ibid., pp. 11-12. See also above, Chapter 5.
37. Ibid., p. 2.
38. Ibid., pp. 7-8.
39. Ibid., pp. 6-12.
40. Ibid., pp. 12-14.
41. Ibid., pp. 13-14.
42. Commission Report, p. 7.
43. Ibid.
44. Ibid., p. 8.
45. Ibid., p. 8.
46. Ibid., p. 26.
47. Commission report, pp. 24, Cf. above p. 64.
48. Ibid., pp. 27-29.

49. Ibid., pars. 239, 240, 244, on pp. 45, 46.
50. George Cole Testimony, April 1948.
51. Ibid.
52. Commission Report, pp. 52-53.
53. Ibid., p. 56.
54. Ibid., p. 56.
55. George Cole Testimony, April 1948.
56. Commission Report, p. 58.
57. Ibid., pp. 72-73.
58. Interviews with Lord Murray (a member of the Commission), May 24, 1966, and Lord Cole in February 1966.
59. See above, pp. 61-62.
60. See below, pp. 75-92.

6. The Independence Route: 1. Africanisation

1. A discussion of African managers is found in records of UAC and Cadburys. See also "History of UAC to 1938" (UAC Records, 1938) and Gold Coast, *A Statement on the Programme of the Africanisation of the Public Service* (Accra, Government Printing Department, 1954), p. 1.
2. *West Africa* (January 11, 1947), p. 272, and January 3, 1948, p. 1306. See also Creech-Jones Papers, Folder 90, "Recruitment and Training for Colonial Services," p. 5, Rhodes House, and Great Britain, *Recruitment and Appointment of Colonial Civil Servants in the United Kingdom,* Cmds. 197 and 198 (1946), and Cmds. 497 (1958) and 1740 (1962).
3. Survey by V. J. Lynch, reported in Gold Coast Legislative Council, *Sessional Papers,* 1944.
4. Gold Coast, *A Statement on the Programme of the Africanisation of the Public Service,* pp. 4-11, quotations from p. 4.
5. Ibid, pp. 10-11. See below, note 10, for references.
6. District Agent, Lagos, 8 August 1938 (Rawlings to Winter on Senior African Staff), p. 3. Holts Records file 8 (now located at Rhodes House, Oxford). See also Richard Symonds, *The British and Their Successors* (London, Faber and Faber, 1966).
7. Letter from H. L. Rawlings to all District Agents in Nigeria, Accra, and Duala, October 30, 1940. Holts Records file 8; Administrative Staff (now located at Rhodes House, Oxford).
8. Pannell, April 10, 1945, "African Managers on the Coast Organisation," File 54, Holts Records, 6 pp., Rhodes House. See also A. C. Walter, and interview with W. T. Gates, Holts, May 1966. Also Philip Curtin, *The Image on Africa* (Madison, Wisc., University of Wisconsin Press, 1964).
9. Interviews with Peter Canham, March 1966; Lord Carrington, July 1968; and Basil Bolt, New Zealand Foreign Office, July 1969.
10. David Kimble, *A Political History of Ghana* (Oxford, Clarendon Press, 1963), pp. 87, 90-95, 538-539, quotations pp. 90, 93, 95, and 538.
11. From manager of Holts to District Agents, "African Managerial Staff," December 7, 1948, p. 1., Holts Records folder 8(vi), "Managerial Staff," Rhodes House.

12. Gold Coast, *A Statement on the Programme of Africanisation of the Public Service*, pp. 4, 10, esp. par. 59.
13. Manager of Holts, december 7, 1948.
14. From Manager John Holt to all District Agents, "African Managerial Staff," December 10, 1948, Holts Records no. 77, Rhodes House.
15. District Agent, Kano, April 1, 1944, "Handing Over Notes," p. 4, Holts Records.
16. *Internal Annual Report*, 1955, now located at Rhodes House.
17. Interviews with E. R. Baines (UAC Ghana, 1938-63), February 9, 1966; with J. O. T. Agyeman, Ghana National Trading Corporation, July 1966; Sir Patrick FitzGerald, July 1966; and Jack More, Manager, Accra UAC, July 1966. *"History of UAC"* (typescript, 1938, in UAC files in London). Discussions of a secondary system and universal education can be found in *The Manchester Guardian*, November 7, 1951; *Ashanti Pioneer* (Kumasi), August 30, 1951; and *The Times*, June 5, 1951.
18. Letter on House of Commons paper (carbon copy) from A. Creech-Jones to Mr. Mellor, UAC (no date on letter), Rhodes House, Box 4, folder 4, items 33-36.
19. Ibid., item 36.
20. Harrigan report.
21. United Africa Company, April 25, 1947 (in UAC records in Accra files).
22. "UAC Testimony to the Commission on the Disturbances," 1948, UAC Accra Files, item 15, p. 4.
23. UAC, 1948, ibid.
24. Ibid.
25. Ibid.
26. Colin Legum, Institute of Commonwealth Studies, University of London, March 18, 1958.
27. J. O. T. Agyeman, note 17, above and interviews with A. R. Aman, (with UAC and related companies from 1922 to 1965). July 28, 1966. See also *West Africa*, November 6, 1948, p. 1125.
28. *The Bournville Works Magazine* (February 1945), p. 24; Cadbury files, BWA minutes, November 3, 1949, and April 10, 1951. See also comments from W. R. Feaver, July 21, 1970.
29. *The Bournville Works Magazine*, (February 1945), pp. 24, 28.
30. Notes of B. J. Silk, Agricultural Training Centre, Kumasi, (1946-1951), p. 6, Rhodes House.
31. Cadbury files, BWA minutes, "Report of Season 1943-44."
32. Ibid., Report, 1946-47.
33. Ibid., "General Manager's Report, 1949-1950."
34. Comments from W. R. Feaver, July 21, 1970.
35. BWA Minutes, July 3, 1951.
36. "General Manager's report, 1956-57."
37. CAST Department of Training and Welfare, Akwatia, Ghana, May 1963.
38. Interview with R. W. Ashworth, CAST, March 30, 1966.
39. Consolidated African Selection Trust Ltd. (Akwatia, Ghana), "Memorandum for Submission to Concessions Commission of Enquiry, 1958," pp. 5-6. Certainly by the mid sixties the housing and other facilities available to the Ghanaian and small expatriate staff were available according to position on staff, whether expatriate or

144 *British Business and Ghanaian Independence*

Ghanaian. The facilities for various employees were more varied than at Ashanti Goldfields. "Observations at Akwatia," July 1966.
40. Interview with Colonel Bean, July 1966.
41. Interviews with General Spears, June 1966, W. M. Jones, Ashanti Goldfields, Obuasi, July 1966. The most junior of the senior staff since 1952 is a shift boss. In 1966, 22 shift bosses were Ghanaians. Letter from W. M. Jones, August 11, 1966.
42. See above, pp. 75-77, 143 note 22.
43. General review of the firms' records and discussions with various officials lead to these conclusions.
44. Creech-Jones Papers, Rhodes House, Box 3, Folder 9, a-f.51. Letter from Kwame Nkrumah, August 15, 1951.
45. Interview with C. H. Wilson, Jesus College, Cambridge, November 1965.
46. David Williams, editor of *West Africa,* indicated some reasons for disagreement with this description, but indicated that firms would not now remember (Interview, November 1965). The major exception was most often remembered in regard to some activities of the Ashanti Goldfields' chairman. See Gamman-Cooper visit to the Gold Coast in various issues of *West Africa,* 1949-51.
47. See discussion of Africanisation and conditions for implementation of such policies in Fred G. Burke and Peter L. French, "Bureaucracy and Africanization," in *Frontiers of Development Administration,* ed. Fred W. Riggs, Durham, N.C., Duke University Press, 1971), pp. 538-555. These authorities state that generally, indigenous people become concerned about this employment after independence. In Ghana the rise in expectations of the indigenous people for Africanisation began to occur before independence, during the decade when the Government was controlled by Africans.
48. Frederic Hunter, "Africanization," *Christian Science Monitor* (October 18, 1969), p. 10. See also Bourret, Kimble, and Crowder.

7. The Independence Route: 2. The Polity and the Economy

1. David Kimble, *A Political History of Ghana,* pp. 404-553. Austin, *Politics in Ghana 1946-1960,* Bourret, *Ghana,* pp. 203-220. Crowder, *West Africa Under Colonial Rule,* esp. pp. 271-512.
2. Commission of Enquiry into Disturbances in the Gold Coast (Watson Commission), *Report* (HMPO, 1948), Colonial no. 231. *Report to His Excellency the Governor by the Committee on Constitutional Reform* (Coussey Commission) (HMPO, 1949), Colonial no. 248.
3. Interview with Sir Alan Burns, September 14, 1965.
4. Ibid., and "Report on Constitutional Matters," from J. A. R. Williams, General Manager, Gold Coast, Holts Records, file no. 421 (March 7, 1952), 311.
5. Mr. Wigg, a Labour MP, also made statements on the efforts to increase self-government in the Gold Coast and on General Spears, support of the MP's travel to the Gold Coast. See the *Daily Telegraph,* October 17,

1950; *West Africa,* autumn 1950; and reports in the *Financial Times,* February 16, March 7, 21, 1951.

6. Letter from General Spears, in the *Financial Times,* March 21, 1951. See also David Gammans' report, "What Next in the Gold Coast?" *Financial Times,* February 16, 1951.

7. Interview, David Williams, editor of *West Africa,* November 1965.

8. *West Africa,* 1951. Interview, James Griffiths, August 1966.

9. Cadburys records, the West Africa Committee Minutes from 1935 to 1957. UAC, George Cole's testimony before the Watson Commission, 1948. Interview, Professor J. H. Richardson, Accra and Eastern Province (Gold Coast), Chamber of Commerce. October 30, 1944. *Report* of the Commission on the Civil Service of the Gold Coast, 1950-51 (Gold Coast, 1951), no. IV of 1951. Also UAC, "Special Announcement," *Nigerian Citizen,* November 5, 1948.

10. Memorandum from A. C. Walker, Manager, Coast Administration Department, John Holt and Company, January 31, 1952.

11. Ibid.

12. Creech-Jones papers, Rhodes House: Box 12, Folders 58, 60; Box 19, folder 95, "Labour and Trade Unions in the Colonies," 1937-58; Box 23, folder 106, "Cooperation in Colonies," 1944-64. Fabian Colonial Research Bureau, pamphlets and various articles in *Empire* and *Venture* (1938-39), periodicals now located at Rhodes House. See also Fabian Society, *The Fabian Society Colonial Essays* (London, George Allen and Unwin, 1945).

13. Interviews, James Griffiths and Sir Alan Burns, August 1966 and September 25, 1965, Creech-Jones papers. Ian Davies, *African Trades Unions* (Harmondsworth, Penguin, 1966), Rhodes House. Rolf Gerritsen, "The Evolution of the Ghana Trades Union Congress under the Convention People's Party," *Transactions of the History Society of Ghana,* 13 (1972), 230-244.

14. *The Times,* November 2, 1951. "Gold Coast Yields Much besides Gold," *New York Times,* August 19, 1951. Interviews and Records, Ashanti Goldfields, Obuwasi, July 1966.

15. News release for October 7, 1952, in Colin Legum's collection.

16. Question in Parliament on April 30, 1917, by Mr. Trevelyan and answered by Mr. Long; see Cartland Papers. Also in the same papers, extract from Enclosure I to Gold Coast Conference, October 10, 1931.

17. General Considerations of the Birim District 1937-38, Cartland Papers, p. 38.

18. Commission of Enquiry into Concessions, *Report* (Gold Coast, 1958), Hearings, 1958. The Concessions Ordinance provided regulations for the lease of mineral rights.

19. Chamber of Mines to the Commission of Enquiry, August 27, 1958.

20. "A Memorandum Submitted by the Ghana Diamond Winners' Association," June 25, 1958.

21. "Memorandum for Submission to Concessions Commission of Enquiry," 1958 by CAST Akwatia, Ghana. Also interview with J. E. F. Knight, May 19, 1966.

22. Consolidation African Selection Trust, Ltd, *Departments of Training and Welfare,* Akwatia, Ghana, September 1962 (mimeographed report), p. 8.

146   *British Business and Ghanaian Independence*

23. "Memorandum for Submission to Concessions Commision of Enquiry."

24. "Summary of Commission of Enquiry into Concessions Recommendations with Government's Comments and Proposed Actions by Governement," files of CAST (London).

25. Ibid., p. 2.

26. Ibid.

27. Ibid., p. 3.

28. Meeting on food shortage with the Minister, Nii Bonnee III, and Messrs, FitzGerald, Alema, Kjin, Tachie-Menson, Abu Bekr, Ferguson, Roach, Pullan, Woode, and Agyarko. Five-page memorandum. Holts Records (first page missing); quotation from p. 5.

29. Minutes of the West African Committee, Cadburys, from 1935. References to methods of controlling swollen shoot disease appear throughout these minutes to 1965. "Control of Swollen Shoot Disease of Cocoa ... in the Eastern Province: History," to 1948, in C. L. Skidmore Collection, Rhodes House.

30. Meeting with the Colonial Secretary, 1945, reported in Holts Records Box 421B(ii).

31. Minutes of meeting, Accra and Eastern Province (Gold Coast) Chamber of Commerce (October 30, 1944), p. 3.

32. "The Takoradi-Axim Forest District," September 1948, D. C. Duff papers, Rhodes House.

33. "Summary of the Report of the Commission of Enquiry into Concessions," 1958 (see note 18, above).

34. UAC references indicated in note 41, below, items 39-42.

35. Interview with James Griffiths, August 1966.

36. Report of House of Commons Debate on July 13, 1943, in report of an interview by Col. The Right Honourable Oliver Stanley, Secretary of State for the Colonies to Deputation from the Association of West Africa Merchants, September 12, 1943, Lagos. Holts files, folder 536 (September 23, 1943), p. 1.

37. Ibid., p. 6.

38. Basil Bolt, in the Colonial Service on the Coast beginning 1948, interview, August, 6 1969. Bolt was appointed the New Zealand High Commissioner to Malaysia in 1975.

39. *Financial Times,* July 27, 1951, "74M, Development Plan for Gold Coast" on the Volta River Project, and discussions with aluminum companies in the United States and Great Britain.

40. Interviews : with James Griffiths, Secretary of State for the Colonies 1950-51, in August 1966; with Sir Gordon Hadow, Colonial Administration in the Gold Coast, on February 23, 1966; and with Peter Canham, formerly of the Gold Coast Colonial Service, in March 1966.

41. "Memorandum submitted to the Commission of Enquiry by the United Africa Company Limited" (April 30, 1948), item 39, UAC records now in Ghana.

42. Ibid., p. 10, item 40.

43. Ibid., p. 11.

44. Ibid., items 41, 42.

45. W. H. Beeton, District Officer in Kumasi, diary, April 1947. See also

report on dinner with Nana Sir Tsibu Darku, *Financial Times*, March 1948.
46. Letter on House of Commons paper (carbon copy) from A. Creech-Jones to Mr. Mellor, UAC 9 (no date on letter), in Rhodes House collection, Box 4, folder 4, items 33-36. Mr. Creech-Jones's letter must have been written after his return from a visit to West Africa in 1947. Mr. Creech-Jones was in the Gold Coast and visiting Kumasi in April 1947 (see records of W. H. Beeton then a District Officer) in his collection).
47. Ibid.
48. Ibid., items 35-36.
49. Ibid.

8. Post-Independence: Development Policies

1. Letter from W. R. Feaver, July 1970.
2. *New York Times,* January 15, 1972. *West Africa,* January 1972, and January 27, 1975, pp. 106-108, 117.
3. Bauer, *West African Trade* (2nd ed., London, Routledge and Kegan Paul, 1963). See also, for sources on British business, A. G. Hopkins, "Imperial Business in Africa, Part I: Sources," *Journal of African History,* 17 (1976), pp. 29-48.
4. Gold Coast Ordinance no. 16 of 1947.
5. P. T. Bauer and B. S. Yamey, *Markets, Market Control and Market Reform* (London, Weidenfield and Nicolson, 1968), pp. 177-200.
6. Tony Killick, "Economics of Cocoa," in Walter Birmingham, *et al., A Study of Contemporary Ghana* (London, George Allen and Unwin, 1966), Vol. 2, pp. 367-70.
7. Letter from W. R. Feaver, July 1970. Notes on interview with Sir Eric Tansley, formerly agent in London office of the Cocoa Marketing Company, February and April 1966. W. R. Feaver, "Collection and Marketing of Cocoa in Producing Countries," in *Agricultural Producers and Their Markets,* ed. T. K. Warley (Oxford, Basil Blackwell, 1967). Tony Killick, "Sectors of the Economy," in Birmingham, Vol. 2, pp. 248-249. For information on earlier arrangements, see Bauer, *West African Trade,* and "The Marketing Boards and the Licensed Buying Agents," in the United Africa Company's *Statistical and Economic Review* (September 14, 1954), pp. 1-6.
8. For a table on prices see Birmingham, Vol, 2, 248-249, and Ghana Cocoa Marketing Board, *Reports,* 1961-66.
9. Cocoa Marketing Board, tables on Reserves of Board from 1947 to 1966 (typescript), July 1966.
10. Letter from W. R. Feaver, July 1970.
11. Interviews with various firms' management personnel, esp. W. R. Feaver, Cadburys, spring 1966, and Ian Bolt and W. T. Gates, John Holt and Company, May 1966.
12. Government of Ghana, "Report of the Committee of Enquiry on the Local Purchasing of Cocoa" (July 23, 1966), pp. 268-284. Members of the Committee were J. C. de Graft-Johnson (chm.), F. R. Kankam-Buadu of the State Cocoa Marketing Board, Kwaku Bugyei Mitim of

the Co-op Bank, J. D. Popplewell (Cadburys), and Patrick Kofi Agbah (Secretary).

13. *West Africa* (January 17, 1970), p. 78; (June 18, 1973), p. 817; (September 10, 1973), p. 1280.
14. Letter from W. R. Feaver, July 1970.
15. *New York Times,* January 14, 15, 1972. Cf. the *London Times,* February–August 1966; *West Africa,* February, 1975; and State Cocoa Marketing Board, *Report,* 1975.
16. *West Africa* (February 21, 1970), p. 199; and Government of Ghana *Highlights of the Year, 1970,* pp. 2, 16. See also notes in last chapter about the firms' participation in development; Dennis Austin, *Politicians and Soldiers in Ghana, 1966-72* (London, Frank Cass, 1975); and *Ghana Observed* (Manchester University Press, 1976).
17. United Africa Company, *Statistical and Economic Review,* April 28, 1963. Interviews with J. L. Pedler, January and May 1966.
18. Interviews with Ian Holt and W. T. Gates, May 1966.
19. Government of Ghana, *Highlights of the Year, 1970,* pp. 2, 7-9.
20. Ibid., and *West Africa,* 1961.
21. *West Africa* (February 1, 1969), p. 127.
22. *Ghanaian Times,* January 15, 1972.
23. Government of Ghana, *Highlights of the Year, 1970,* pp. 2, 7-9, 10-11, 13-14, and 16.
24. Ibid.
25. Interviews, Richard Quashie, Director, CAST, July 1966. *West Africa* (February 11, 1970), p. 222; (January 27, 1975), p. 117.
26. J. F. Milburn, "Cocoa Marketing in Ghana," in *Cocoa Production,* ed. John Simmons (New York, Praeger, 1976).
27. R. A. Kotey, "The Organisation of the Internal Marketing of Cocoa," paper at Cocoa Economics Research Conference, Legon, April 9-12, 1973. J. C. de Graft-Johnson, "Co-operative Marketing of Cocoa in Ghana, 1929-1972," ibid.
28. J. F. Milburn, "Marketing Boards in New Zealand," paper in draft, 1975.
29. International Cocoa Agreement, 1972 (Geneva, October 20, 1972), entered into force provisionally, June 30, 1973.
30. *West Africa* (January 18, 1973, June 18, 1973), pp. 5, 47, 817; (September 10, 1973), p. 1280.
31. Presentation to May 28, 1975, meeting of the Organisation for Economic Co-operation and Development. *Economist* (June 14, 1975), p. 49. *Times Magazine* (May 26, 1975), p. 57. For commodity prices, see the *Economist* (June 14, 1975), p. 49, and the *Australian* (July 15, 1975).

9.   *The Contribution of Expatriate Firms*

1. See types of exceptions mentioned above, Chapter 7, pp. 94-95.
2. See above Chapter 8, pp. 113-114.

INDEX

Accra, 12, 16, 24, 71, 84; Brewery, 102; Central, 95; Committee on Cocoa Marketing, 26-27, 44-45, 50. *See also* Chambers of Commerce
Acheampong, Colonel I. K., 110
Achimota College, 6, 8, 30, 73-75, 78, 81, 92; endowment, 95
Acquaye, A. D. K., 58
Administration, Coastal, 28, 93
Advances (cash), 12, 16, 17
African and Eastern Trade Corporation, 4
African Produce Buyers, 34-35
African Timber and Plywood Ltd., 101
Africanisation 69-92, 122-123; Commissioner for, 70; Ghanaians in economic and political positions, 40, 63-65; in Civil Service, 95; policy, 70. *See also* Ashanti Goldfields, Barclays DCO, Cadburys, CAST, Holts, UAC
African Company of Merchants, 6
African Morning Post, 21, 47
African Timber and Plywood Company, 66
Africans, 69-73, 77, 81-83, 90-92; clerical staff, 71-72, 75, 85, 89-91; ethics, 73; in Administration, 6-7, 8; in Assembly, 7, 8; in British firms, 30, 69-92; in Legislative Council, 6, 62-63; in management, 73-80, 84-87, 89-92; language, 72; representation, 93; rulers, 6; storekeepers, 76; students to America and to the United Kingdom, 63. *See also* Farmers
Agreements, trade: cocoa, 13-17, 21; palm oil, 13. *See also* Buying Agreement
Agricultural Development Corporation Board, 105
Agricultural Training Centre, Kumasi, 81
Agriculture, Department of, 36, 37, 99; Director, 46
Agriculture, Ministry of, Produce Inspection Division, 107

Agyeman, J. O. T., 75
Air mail service, 28
Ajetey, Sergeant, 7
Akan, 6
Akosombo Hydroelectric Power State, 112
Akwatia, 86
Allen, A. D. W., 58
Aluminium, 66, 101
Anokwalefo (pseudonym for contributor to *African Morning Post*), 21
Apeadu, Kafo, 3
Arden-Clarke, Sir Charles (Governor), 95
Asantehene (Paramount Chief), 6
Ashanti, 6, 17; Corporation, 97; Territory, 65. *See also* Farmers and Kumasi
Ashanti Committee. *See* Kumasi Committee on Cocoa Marketing
Ashanti Goldfields, 87-89, 111; and Erroll, F. J., 97; expatriates and Ghanaian personnel, 88; and Spears, Major-General Sir Edward, 94, 111
Assembly, House of (Nigeria), 95; Legislative, 7-9
Association of British Chambers of Commerce. *See* Chambers of Commerce
Association of Cocoa Manufacturers, 5
Association of West African Merchants (AWAM), 5, 33, 36-38, 41, 49, 59-61, 68; advisory committee, 36-37; Cocoa Sub-Committee of, 34, 49
Atta, Nana Ofori. *See* Ofori Atta, Hon. Nana Sir
Auchinlech, Mr. (Director of Agriculture, 1939), 46
Avoidance of Discrimination Act, 95
AWAM. *See* Association of West African Merchants

Bacon-making, 102
Bank of Ghana (Central Bank), 111

149